江苏高校优势学科建设工程资助项目

A Project Funded by the Priority Academic Program Development of Jiangsu Higher Education Institutions

Legal Translation

法律翻译

董晓波 于银磊 / 著

图书在版编目（CIP）数据

法律翻译 / 董晓波，于银磊著 . —北京：北京大学出版社，2020.4
ISBN 978-7-301-31306-0

Ⅰ.①法… Ⅱ.①董… ②于… Ⅲ.①法律—英语—翻译 Ⅳ.① D9

中国版本图书馆 CIP 数据核字 (2020) 第 048765 号

书　　名	法律翻译 FALÜ FANYI
著作责任者	董晓波　于银磊　著
责任编辑	刘文静
标准书号	ISBN 978-7-301-31306-0
出版发行	北京大学出版社
地　　址	北京市海淀区成府路 205 号　100871
网　　址	http://www.pup.cn　新浪微博: @ 北京大学出版社
电子信箱	liuwenjing008@163.com
电　　话	邮购部 010-62752015　发行部 010-62750672　编辑部 010-62754382
印刷者	北京鑫海金澳胶印有限公司
经销者	新华书店 720 毫米 ×1020 毫米　16 开本　10.75 印张　400 千字 2020 年 4 月第 1 版　2020 年 4 月第 1 次印刷
定　　价	52.00 元

未经许可，不得以任何方式复制或抄袭本书之部分或全部内容。
版权所有，侵权必究
举报电话：010-62752024 电子信箱：fd@pup.pku.edu.cn
图书如有印装质量问题，请与出版部联系，电话：010-62756370

Introduction

With the promotion of Belt and Road Initiative, China is increasingly participating in international political, economic and cultural communications. Legal translation plays a more and more important role in international communication and offers Chinese wisdom and a Chinese approach to solving global problems.

This book presents an overview of legal translation, and provides a theoretical and practical guidance for the study and practice of legal translation. It adopts an interdisciplinary approach, which combines linguistic and legal theories with translation practice. In short, this book is divided into two parts. The first five chapters present the theoretical aspects of legal translation, attempting to address the following questions. What are the linguistic features of legal language? What are the major factors making legal translation difficult and challenging? What are the theories and principles for legal translation? What is required of the legal translators? The last five chapters are practice-oriented, focusing on the practical aspects of legal translation. It illustrates the strategies for translating the legal terminologies, fixed expressions in legal texts and certain legal documents.

This book is to provide a guide to the multidisciplinary nature of legal translation. It could be used by university students majoring in English or Translation, and it could be of interest for students, scholars, professionals of Law.

Contents

Chapter One   General Introduction 1

Chapter Two   Law, Language and Translation 5

    Language and Law 5
    Legal Language 6
    Legal Texts 15

Chapter Three   Legal English 22

    History of Legal English 23
    Lexical Features of Legal English 28
    Syntactic Features of Legal English 39

Chapter Four   Legal Translation and Equivalence 46

    Factors Influencing Legal Translation 47
    Legal Translational Equivalence: Possibility and Impossibility 61

Chapter Five   Theories and Principles for Legal Translation 63

    Functional Equivalence Theory 64
    Dual Equivalence and Ideal Equivalence: Application of Functional
        Equivalence Theory to Legal Translation 68
    Basic Principles for Legal Translation 73

Chapter Six Legal Terminological Issues in Translation 82

Translating Legal Concepts 82
Focusing on the Meaning of Legal Terminology 84
Problems in the Translation of Legal Terminology in China 86

Chapter Seven Translation Competence and Techniques for Legal Translation 91

Translation Competence of the Legal Translator 91
Translation Techniques for Legal Translation 95

Chapter Eight Translation on the Programmed Structures in Legal Texts 111

Strategies for Translating Fuzzy Expression 111
Strategies for Translating Sentences with "的" Structure 119
Translation of Some Typical Expressions 123

Chapter Nine Translation on Marketing Agreements 129

Introduction 129
Law Notes 133
Expressions Commonly Used in Marketing Agreements 134
Sample Translation on a Marketing Agreement 138

Chapter Ten Translation on Breach of Contract Claim 146

Introduction 146
A Claim Form 147
Law Notes 151
Sample Translation on a Chinese Complaint 152

Bibliography 156

Chapter One

General Introduction

The last two decades have witnessed a huge increase in international exchange and communication, to a degree that would have never been imagined. The nations of the world have become so interdependent that no country can develop by closing its door. Law has a vital part to play in reinforcing communication between nations and peoples. As a result of the free movement of people, goods and capital throughout the world, legal translation affects all of us in one way or another. International trade, for example, couldn't function without legal translation. With the promotion of Belt and Road Initiative, China is increasingly participating in international political, economic and cultural communications. It is obvious that translation is integral to the interaction in law and other spheres between different peoples and countries. Ever since its accession to the World Trade Organization (WTO) in 2001, China has been brought into overall environment of globalization so that it can no longer be confined to its own legal jurisdictions and linguistic groups. The demand for legal translation is on the increase owing to globalization, especially when we are working to build a community with a shared future for mankind. There is an urgent need to introduce advanced legislative ideas and successful judicial practices from developed countries so as to perfect its own legal systems, as well as to enhance its international competitiveness by introducing Chinese legislative texts to the whole world. All of these can't be done without legal translation.

Legal translation has played a very important part in the contact between

法律翻译
LEGAL TRANSLATION

different peoples and different cultures in history, and is playing an even more important role in our increasingly globalized world. On the one hand, it is important for us to see the different consequences and effects that translation can have on the working and development of law. The choice of words and different methods of translation can have a long-lasting impact on law. Translations of legal texts lead to legal effects and may even bring peace or cause warfare. Concerned about the severe consequences arising from past translation errors in treaties, Kuner (1991: 953) comments, "The growing trend toward providing authentic texts of treaties in four or more languages poses dangers to the peace and stability of the international order." On the other hand, legal translation is the product of human exchange, through which learning, referencing and assimilation of foreign advanced law system become possible. Thus we cannot deny the assertion that it has greatly accelerated the social development, especially the process of modernization of legal system. Just as Zhang Wenxian (2005), a famous jurist puts it, "Legal translation is an important component of Chinese legal reform. It is an element task, without which Chinese legal education couldn't be thriving today." Meanwhile, "legal translation offers Chinese wisdom and a Chinese approach to solving global problems," said Dong Xiaobo (2018). More importantly, owing to the all-embracing contents of law, legal translation covers a wide range of subjects and thus enriches the languages, cultures and human experience as a whole.

Given its important role in the institutional and intellectual development in society, legal translation deserves close scrutiny. This fact, unfortunately, is not often acknowledged, in particular in the development of law. Although translations of legal texts are among the oldest and the most important in the world, legal translation has long been neglected in both translation and legal studies. Far from being recognized as an independent discipline, legal translation is regarded by translation theorists merely as one of the many subject areas of special-purpose translation, a branch of translation studies often snubbed for its alleged inferiority. (Sarcevic 1997:1) Along with the trend of globalization and the development of intercultural communications, both translators and legal scholars have been pondering over the problem of legal translation. The former have been attempting to address the problem mainly from a linguistic angle, while the latter trying to approach it from a forensic point of view.

In China, there are many well-known scholars who have devoted themselves to doing systematic research on the legal translation. To name just a few, Chen Zhongcheng (1998a) in his book, *Window on Legal Translation*, discusses the diction and syntax features of legal English as well as some typical mistakes and problems in legal translation. Du Jinbang (2004) elaborates the relation between language and law in *Forensic Linguistics*. Li Kexing and Zhang Xinhong (2006), analyses the types of legal texts and the linguistic characteristics in *Legal Texts and Legal Translation*. They also talk about the status of legal translation and provide series of practical techniques for legal translators.

In recent years, the National People's Congress, the Legal Affairs Office of the State Council and the Legal Affairs Office of all the provinces have set up professional teams to translate the laws, regulations and rules. The research on the problems and solutions of legal translation springs up. Scholars like Du Jinbang et al. (2004), Dong Xiaobo (2011), Qu Wensheng (2012), Li Jin and Dong Xiaobo (2015) all stress the importance of the consistency and standardization of Legal Translation. As to the legal English education program in China, an increasing number of universities and colleges have offered Legal English courses, such as Guangdong University of Foreign Studies, Zhongnan University of Economics and Law, Nanjing Normal University, Hebei Normal University etc. Scholars gradually turn their attention to macroscopic problems of legal translation like the compilation and writing of textbooks, the teaching philosophy and practices, the training of interdisciplinary talents. (See Zhao Junfeng and Luo Wenqi 2012, Li Fengxia et al. 2015, Xu Duo 2017, Zhang Falian 2018)

These demonstrate the fruitful achievements and rapid development of the studies on legal translation in China; however, most of the studies focus on

questions of terminology or confined to the empirical study of practicing, while textual and pragmatic considerations tend to be ignored. Moreover, there appears to be no consensus among linguists and lawyers on acceptable translation techniques, let alone on a theoretical approach to legal translation. Obviously, the research on legal translation leaves much room for improvement. Many theoretical problems, together with practical problems are still to be settled.

Chapter Two

Law, Language and Translation

Legal translation is a special and specialized kind of translation, which involves the translation of texts within the field of law and often produces not only linguistic effect but also legal force. As is noted, the translation of legal texts of any kind, from statute laws to contracts to courtroom testimony, is a practice that stands at the crossroads of legal theory, language theory and translation theory. (Joseph 1995:25) As a result, it is essential that legal translators should have a general understanding of the nature of law and legal language and the impact they may have on the translation.

Language and Law

Law, the demonstration of the national power and the guarantee of a stable society, forms the framework within which we manage our daily affairs. It protects the people and the nation and punishes criminals of various types. Laws are coded in languages and concepts that are used to construct the law; language is the carrier of laws and the medium through which laws act. The famous American lawyer, Mellinkoff (1990) once said frankly, "The law is a profession of words." In his opinion, language is the soul of the law.

Law depends upon language, without which law is inconceivable. Laws are written in language, the function of which is not just to express or convey

information and knowledge, but also to direct, influence or modify people's behavior. As is noted by Maley (1994:11),

> In all societies, law is formulated, interpreted and enforced... and the greater part of these different legal process is realized primarily through language. Language is the medium, process and product in the various arenas of the law where legal texts, spoken or written, are generated in the service of regulating social behavior.

Law is closely tied to and constrained by the language that it uses. The close relationship between language and law sets the stage for the growth of legal language, a frontier science with overlap of linguistics and the science of law.

Legal Language

The Concept of Legal Language

Legal language does not qualify as a language in the same way as Chinese, English or French, for example. The term "legal language" originates from the west. It originally refers to the language or part of a certain language used for expressing legal concepts and dealing with litigation and non-litigation legal affairs. Afterwards, it also covers those words and expressions possessing certain legal significance and extends to other language level. Like language for science and technology, financial language, advertising language and so on, legal language belongs to the language for specific purposes. In general, a legal language is a formalized language based on logic rules which differs from the ordinary natural language in vocabulary, morphology, syntax, and semantics, as well as other linguistic features. (Wydick 2005:10)

It is clear to see that legal language is based on ordinary language. For that reason, the grammar and in general, the vocabulary of legal language are the

Chapter Two Law, Language and Translation

same as those of ordinary language. However, legal language is a language for special purposes. This means, first of all, there are a large number of legal terms whose properties vary according to the branches of the law. In addition, the legal languages of different countries and of different periods possess, to a varying degree, characteristics that distinguish them from ordinary written language (e.g., sentence structure). One may speak of a specific legal style. For those reasons, it often occurs that legal language may be incomprehensible from the standpoint of the general public. Just as Tiserma (1999:52) points out,

> Legal language has been called an argot, a dialect, a register, a style, and even a separate language. In fact, it is best described with the relatively new term sublanguage. A sublanguage has its own specialized grammar, a limited subject matter, contains lexical, syntactic, and semantic restrictions, and allows "deviant" rules of grammar that are not acceptable in the standard language. However we describe it, legal language is a complex collection of linguistic habits that have developed over many centuries and that lawyers have learned to use quite strategically.

Legal language is often characterized as a technical language, which is to say a language used by professionals. It is accurate to a certain extent. Legal language is, first and foremost, used by lawyers and judges. Nevertheless, when members of the lay public are involved as parties, experts, or jurors, they will inevitably be confronted with legal language, which in many cases will create a need for some kind of explanation or translation (as when jury instructions try to explain legal concepts in ordinary language). At the same time, it seems natural to say that a citizen who, for example, writes his own will following a model form is using legal language. Still more important, by contrast with most other languages for special purposes, the target of messages transmitted in legal language often consists of the whole population, certain layers of the population, or a number of particular citizens. For example, a law normally requires compliance of all the people, while a

court judgment relates, first and foremost, to the parties involved in the case. Thus, legal language is not an instrument aimed solely at internal communication within the legal profession.

Use of legal language is notable for the fact that it is very widespread: it governs all areas of social life, and it can, through intertextuality, be combined with language from any and every domain. Furthermore, legal language is very old, which is not necessarily the case with most other languages for special purposes. This is why, historically, it has shaped the ordinary language of various countries, and in a significant way. However, this is not a matter of a unique historical phenomenon. Even today, legal language still influences ordinary language.

Legal language nowadays can be comprehended both in a narrow sense and a broad sense. In a narrow sense, legal language merely refers to legislative language used in normative documents, while in a broad sense, it refers to legislative, executive and judicial language. By legislative language we mean the formal and concrete language used in legal provisions, such as country's constitutions, civil law, criminal law, regulations and other normative pronouncements which permit, command, or prohibit a certain cause of conduct. Executive language is defined as the language used in the process of implementing the law, such as in the process of detention. Judicial language refers to language employed in the courtroom, such as judicial decisions, briefs, appeals, petitions and remarks by judges, lawyers, witnesses and other participants, including both the written and spoken forms. For example, the spoken judicial language may include the language used by lawyers in courtroom disputes, and speeches delivered by plaintiff, defendants, judges, etc.

In this book, we will basically focus on the legislative language because legislative language emerges in the written form, which is more compact and dense, while executive and judicial language involves spoken forms, which tends to be less formal. Besides, the legislative part is the most typical and therefore the most representative part of legal language.

Chapter Two Law, Language and Translation

Linguistic Features of Legal Language[1]

Legal language, as we said earlier, is a type of register, that is, a variety of languages appropriate to the legal situations of use. It possesses a number of special characteristics in comparison with ordinary language. These characteristics are to some extent in evidence in the same way in all legal languages (e.g., Chinese, English, French). The following is an overview of the main linguistic features of legal language.

Precision and Fuzziness

Precision and accuracy are regarded as fundamental characteristics of legal language. The seriousness of legal language makes it essential to avoid any inaccurate and unclear expressions, because inaccuracy may lead to ambiguity, ambiguity to misunderstanding, and further to disputes. To avoid the possibility of arbitrariness, legal rules should be formulated without ambiguity. Therefore, being accurate and precise is the soul of legal language and linguistic clarity is an absolute norm of legislation.

The basic goal of legal language is to transmit legal messages with absolute clarity and without ambiguity. This essentially results from the requirement for legal protection and legal certainty. Hence, legislators are required to make a detailed distinction among words that are interchangeably used by layman. For example, the differences between right and privilege, duty and obligation, jail and prison, residence and domicile, may be of little consequence in daily communication, but extremely significant in legal documents. Only when accurate and precise expressions are adopted in legal language, can legislation provide people with behavioral mode or standard and then the aim of "rule of law" be realized.

---

[1] This part is a rewritten version of *Characteristics of Legal Language in Comparative Legal Linguistics* by Matilla, H. in 2006.

However, fuzziness is the same prominent feature as accuracy in legal language. It is universally acknowledged that no matter how hard we try, it is difficult to express all the specific behavior modes, motivations and results in a successful and comprehensive way just with the limited language symbols. The fact is that fuzziness comes into being inevitably when language is applied to carry an array of information. Legal language, as a part of natural language, is also intrinsically fuzzy.

Fuzzy expressions are usually employed in the legal texts in order to improve the generality of the language, so as to enumerate different situations to the largest extent, for example, to make the case that has never happened before or we cannot foresee solved well. In international relations, linguistic fuzziness may also be a conscious choice in certain negotiating situations. For example, negotiators can leave equivocal an article of an international treaty on which they have not reached agreement. To achieve generality and flexibility, legal language usually adopts words like "appropriate" "acceptable" "reasonable" with the aim to achieve effective communicative function; a term like "appropriate" can change with the times and circumstances. However, if a word is too fuzzy, it will leave many available interpretations open to disputes and thus give great discretion to the judges in the decision-making process. Therefore, generality and flexibility is necessary but should be limited in use because people should know in advance what is legal and what is illegal.

In short, the relationship between the two features—fuzziness and precision is not contradictory but complementary, thus making the law system more complete.

Information Overload

In a modern and highly complex society, the number of legal rules is enormous. To speak of a flood of legal rules aptly sums up the situation. To help stem the tide, legal language should be as concise as possible, to avoid laws and regulations that would otherwise be over-long and unclear. At the same time, legal language should

Chapter Two Law, Language and Translation

avoid over-abstraction, in that way enabling decoding with minimum effort.

Harmonizing these goals is not easy. The key is to know for whom laws are written: experts or citizens? Even laws concerning fundamental questions of citizens' lives are often written for experts because it is experts who are charged with their technical application. Examples include matters of social and fiscal law. In these matters, laws are necessarily highly complex: this is a question of distributive justice, which presupposes highly detailed rules. These rules might even express in language form a mathematical formula relating to the calculation of some welfare allowance or a tax to be paid. This means that social and fiscal laws should be written very compactly, with as high a density of information as possible, to prevent their becoming over-long.

The legislator does not suppose that laws of a technical character are understandable from the standpoint of the general public. As we have seen, the principles of these laws are communicated to citizens by means of short-form bulletins, leaving out the details.

It is easy to understand that the problem caused by the great density of information of legal language concerns not only legislative language. In many civil-law countries like France, the language of judgments is traditionally loaded with messages: it is compact and full of expressions that have the appearance of abridged codes. Today, following criticisms from linguists, judgments in some countries are written in a language closer to ordinary language. However, some scholars have commented that this means, on the one hand, that judgments have become too long, and on the other hand, that their internal logic is weakened: a judgment formulated in ordinary language contains more secondary—even meaningless—elements, impeding transmission of the legal message, than a traditional compact judgment.

Neutrality

In general, legal language today tends to be official and formal. The style of this language is as neutral as possible because the main intention is to have an

effect on the understanding, rather than the feelings, of the reader or listener. This is why one author says that the style of legal language is "cold": it rejects all that is affective and does not include emotional elements. This is why legal texts contain practically no exclamation or question marks. Nor should legal language give rise to irrelevant associations that distract the attention of the reader of the document or discourse in question. The neutrality of legal language is largely guaranteed by the fact that many legal texts (e.g., laws, administrative instructions, on the Continent also judgments) pass through the offices of several commentators and stylists before receiving their final form: they are not from a single hand.

The rigorousness of the requirement for linguistic neutrality varies according to the general culture and traditions of the country in question. In civil-law countries, for example, it is self-evident that a judge should express himself in an absolutely calm and composed way. On this topic, it appears that Anglo-American judges enjoy a far greater freedom. An illustration of this is the dissenting opinion of judge Musmanno, of the Pennsylvania Supreme Court, in the case relating to Henry Miller's work, "Tropic of Cancer" (Tiersma 1999: 140-141):

> "Cancer" is not a book. It is a cesspool, an open sewer, a pit of petrification, a slimy gathering of all that is rotten in the debris of human depravity. And in the center of all this waste and stench, besmearing himself with its foulest defilement, splashes, leaps, cavorts and wallows a bifurcated specimen that responds to the name of Henry Miller... From Pittsburgh to Philadelphia, from Dan to Beersheba, and from the Ramparts of *the Bible* to Samuel Eliot Morison's *Oxford History of the American People*, I dissent.

Objectivisation and Impersonality

As a frozen style, the legal language manifests its authoritativeness and solemnness by employing objective and impersonal expressions. This feature is best proved by the frequent use of the "impersonal construction" which means the

Chapter Two Law, Language and Translation

avoidance of first and second personal pronouns like "I" and "you" (Tiersma 1999). For instance, Article 46 in Criminal Law rules that, "Any criminal who is sentenced to fixed-term imprisonment or life imprisonment shall serve his sentence in prison or another place for the execution." The usage of third person gives an objective impression to the public and guarantees the act in the real practice that the cases are decided in accordance with the legislative authority instead of personal emotions. Other linguistic devices contributing to the objectivity include the passive voice, which is also noticeably used in legal documents. This brings the object of the action into the foreground, giving the actor only a secondary role. This feature is clear to see in all specialist languages, but is a particular highlight in legal matters. In this way, authors of legal texts underline the objectivity of their findings and conclusions.

Both "impersonal constructions" and passive voice create an impression of objectivity and strengthen the authority of law. To sum up, the feature of being objective and impersonal illustrates the essence of the law, that is, to judge every case only by the rule of law and exclude the rule of man.

Sentence Complexity and Diversity of Language Elements

Sentences in legal language are traditionally very long and complicated. This is largely due to force of tradition: legal language involves a language for special purposes of great antiquity whose stylistic elements often stem from Medieval Latin. Even in our times, complicated and useless expressions are added to legal texts, making them more difficult to understand. For example, in the United States there is a fondness for using expressions considered "polished" and "energetic" (Tiersma 1999: 59–60): *at slow speed* instead of *slowly*, *in the event that* instead of *if*, *prior to* instead of *before*, *subsequent to* instead of *after*.

Difficulties of understanding also occur because legal and administrative language places less emphasis on verbs than ordinary language. This is partly explained by the notion according to which a noun gives a more objective impression

than a verb, notably in cases involving findings of fact. The wealth of nouns in legal and administrative texts is accentuated by the fact that these nouns often form phrases (groups of words forming a lexical unit) or notably in some languages, such as German, the Scandinavian languages and so on. This is because a term created to express a new legal concept should also be as transparent as possible, that is, it immediately shows the uninitiated what it is about. If the particular words forming part of the phrase or compound word in question each express an essential feature of the new concept, then such transparency is ensured. The following examples will illustrate: in French, *contrat de transfert de processus technologique, Cour de justice des Communautés européennes* or in German, *Aussagevenveigerungsrecht, Klageerzwingungsverfahren*. These examples show the price of transparency: expressions in legal language are often very heavy.

Further, different language elements mingle in legal language. Firstly, this language contains words from ordinary language used in their ordinary meaning. Secondly, it contains words from ordinary language used in a technical sense. Thirdly, it presents words that are only technical terms. These may be legal terms, or terms from other specialisms. Linguistic research affirms that in legal texts the number of such legal terms that have only a legal meaning is relatively limited in comparison with other specialist languages. The majority of legal terms are words from ordinary language that possess a particular meaning in legal contexts. This is sometimes dangerous: the uninitiated reader imagines having understood the meaning of the term, but in reality the term means something else in legal language.

On the other hand, legal texts always contain terms from other specialisms (e.g., commerce, technology). One illustration is texts produced by organs of the European Union. A directive of the European Communities on agriculture may include terms from law, agronomy, commerce, and technology. A full understanding of such a directive requires knowledge of all these sciences, which deepens the hermetic character of the text.

Chapter Two   Law, Language and Translation

Legal Texts

Classification of Legal Texts

Legal texts can be classified according to different criteria. For instance, Jean-Claude Gémar, divides legal texts into three groups according to the subject-matter, i.e., whether the text regulates public or private affairs. His first group of texts contains laws, regulations, judgments, and international treaties, while the second group consists of contracts, administrative and commercial forms, wills, etc. The third group contains scholarly works. (See also Sarcevic 1997: 17) One major problem with this classification is that many documents that are used in the legal process and translated as such are excluded from classifications, e.g. documents used in court proceedings.

As a type of special-purpose texts, legal texts can also be divided into groups according to their functions. In legal theory, the most widely accepted classification is the bipartite system in which language have two primary functions: regulatory and informative, i.e., prescriptive and descriptive. (Sarcevic 1997: 11) The regulatory group contains legal texts whose function is primarily prescriptive include laws, regulations, codes, contracts, treaties and conventions. Such texts are normative instruments containing rules of conduct or norms. The informative group consists of hybrid texts that are primarily descriptive but also contain prescriptive parts. These include judicial decisions and legal instruments that are used to carry on judicial and administrative proceedings such as actions, pleadings, briefs, appeals, requests, petitions, etc. (Li & Zhang 2006:11)

Accordingly, legal texts may have various communicative purposes. They can be for normative purpose as in the case of laws, statutes and other documents that establish legal facts or create rights and obligations. These are mostly prescriptive. Legal texts can also be for informative purpose as in some legal scholarly works and commentaries, legal advice, correspondence between lawyers, and documents

used in court proceedings. These are mostly descriptive. For legal translators, it is necessary to ascertain the legal status and communicative purpose of the original texts and target texts as these may have impact on translation. For example, the main characteristics of a law are authority and formality, but those of a testimony are reliability and facticity. This book deals primarily with normative texts such as constitutions, statutes, codes, treaties and international conventions, etc.

Tone of Legal Texts

As is known to all, legal texts are formulated in a professional language generally known as the language of the law. Legislative writing is so impersonal that it is independent of whoever the drafter is or the addressee is. The general function of legal texts is regulatory and informative, or to impose obligations and to confer rights. In translation, the tone of a text is the key to its communicative effectiveness, and has to be determined by the translators. Therefore, keeping the tone of legal text in mind does help translators understand the importance of the function of legal text in translation.

The function of legal text plays a crucial role in determining translation strategy and achieving the desired legal effects. It is believed that the correct understanding of legal texts is not only the basis on which the legal translators grasp the intention and for function of the legal text concerned but also the decisive factor to determine its translation criteria and its translation techniques to be employed in achieving the said criteria.

Commands and Requirements

A legal command imposes a duty upon the legal subject to act in a certain manner under given circumstances. Legal commands are mandatory provisions; hence failure to act accordingly is a violation of the law punishable by sanction. The English practice of imposing legal duties by the legal imperative *shall* is a longstanding practice dating back to English translations of Roman law texts. The

Chapter Two Law, Language and Translation

first extant translation of *Magna Carta*, originally in Latin, has been called "an exercise in *shall*."

Example 1: 选出或者罢免人民检察院检察长，须报上级人民检察院检察长提请该级人民代表大会常务委员会批准。

Translation: The election or recall of chief procurators of people's procuratorates shall be reported to the chief procurators of the people's procuratorates at the next higher level for submission to the standing committees of the people's congresses at the corresponding level for approval.

Example 2: If the Buyers fail to notify and/or forward full details within the period specified above, the Buyers shall be deemed to have waived their right to assert any claim.

Translation: 如果买方未能在上述规定的期间内通知和（或）寄出完整的细节，那么买方将被认为放弃提出任何索赔的权利。

Example 3: 一切法律、行政法规和地方性法规都不得同宪法相抵触。一切国家机关和武装力量、各政党和各社会团体、各企业事业组织都必须遵守宪法和法律。一切违反宪法和法律的行为，必须予以追究。

Translation: No law or administrative or local rules and regulations shall contravene the constitution. All state organs, the armed forces, all political parties and public organizations and all enterprises and undertakings must abide by the Constitution and the law. All acts in violation of the Constitution and the law must be investigated.

Permission and Authorization

In addition to imposing duties, legislative texts also confer rights, privileges, and powers on legal subjects in the form of permissions and authorizations. The modal "may" is usually used to express permissions and authorizations in English. While it is agreed that a permission expresses a facultative operation, there are cases where the courts have interpreted a permissive "may" as "shall," thus turning it into a mandatory provision. Although authorizations can be construed as a duty,

such provisions are usually fuzzy as to whether the performance of an authorized act is mandatory.

Permission

Lawyers often say that an act that is not expressively prohibited is permitted. Yet there are a number of explicit permissions. By granting permissions, the legislature limits the number of potential prohibitions. More importantly, the granting of a permission is a means of cancelling a command, requirement, or prohibition or making an exception to a command, requirement, or prohibition.

Authorization

An authorization is a special type of legal speech act in which the permissive *may, shall, have the right/power to, enjoy the right of, be entitled to, be authorized to*, etc. and Chinese expressions "享有……权利""有权……" can be construed as expressing a right. Technically speaking, authorizations confer power upon some person or authority to perform an act which otherwise that person or authority would be without power to perform.

Example 1: 参加农村集体经济组织的劳动者,有权在法律规定的范围内经营自留地、自留山、家庭副业和饲养自留畜。

Translation: Working people who are members of rural economic collective have the right, within the limits prescribed by law, to farm plots of cropland and hilly land allotted for their private use, engage in household sideline production and raise privately owned livestock.

Example 2: If you are currently claiming Income Support, Housing Benefit, Council Tax Credit and Pension Credit you may be entitled to fee remission.

Translation: 如果你现时在申请"收入补助""住房福利""市政会税务信贷"或"养老金信贷",你可以有权获得费用豁免。

Example 3: 当事人依法可以委托代理人订立合同。

Translation: The parties may conclude a contract through an agent in accordance with the law.

Chapter Two Law, Language and Translation

Prohibitions

Prohibitions are legal speech acts with the illocutionary force of forbidding. The most common type of prohibitions are acts that persons and/or an authority are explicitly forbidden to perform and whose performance is punishable by sanction. In view of their obligatory nature, such prohibitions are regarded as negative commands: X is obliged to refrain from performing act A; if X performs act A, he/she/it is subject to punishment. As the very opposite of commands, prohibitions are expressed in English with the negation *shall/may/must not, be prohibited/not allowed, be not obliged/permitted* and in Chinese with "严禁""禁止""不得""不能", etc.

Example 1: 判决宣告以前一人犯数罪的，除判处死刑和无期徒刑的以外，应当在总和刑期以下、数刑中最高刑期以上，酌情决定执行的刑期；但是管制最高不能超过三年，拘役最高不能超过一年，有期徒刑总和刑期不满三十五年的，最高不能超过二十年，总和刑期在三十五年以上的，最高不能超过二十五年。

Translation: For a criminal who commits several crimes before a judgment is pronounced, unless he is sentenced to death or life imprisonment, his term of punishment shall be decided in such a way that it may not exceed the total of the terms for all the crimes and must be longer than the maximum term for any one of the crimes, depending on the circumstances of each case. However, the term of public surveillance may not exceed three years, the term of criminal detention may not exceed one year, and fixed-term imprisonment may not exceed 20 years if the sum of terms of fixed imprisonment is less than 35 years or may not exceed 25 years if the sum of terms is 35 years or more.

Example 2: 禁止证券交易内幕信息的知情人和非法获取内幕信息的人利用内幕信息从事证券交易活动。

Translation: Persons possessing inside information relating to securities trading and persons obtaining such information unlawfully are prohibited from making use of such inside information in securities trading activities.

Example 3: 没收财产是没收犯罪分子个人所有财产的一部分或者全部。在判处没收财产的时候，不得没收属于犯罪分子家属所有或者应有的财产。

Translation: Confiscation of property refers to the confiscation of part or all of the property personally owned by a criminal. When a sentence of confiscation of property is imposed, property that the criminal's family member owns or should own shall not be subject to confiscation.

Translation of Legal Texts

As stated above, a legal text is vested with legal effects and intended to serve a specific function. For the most part, modern translation theorists no longer regard translation as a mechanical process of transcoding one language into another. Nor is a text regarded as "a string of words and structures to be converted into a string of equivalents" (Snell-Hornby 1988:75). Primarily under the influence of German scholars, the main emphasis in general translation theory has shifted from language to the cultural aspects of translation.

Legal translation involves the transfer of a message from a legal text producer to a receiver. Lawyers are aware that, in order for plurilingual communication to be effective in the law, one must preserve the unity of the single instrument, as it is called in international law. (Tabory 1980:195) In other words, legal communication can be successful only if the legal translator is able to translate the message into linguistic code that is identical in meaning. Thus, legal translation was largely regarded as a means of transferring meaning by linguistic transcoding. This has long been taken to mean that the goal of legal translation is to preserve the meaning of the original texts, which consists in reproducing, transferring, or reconstructing the meaning of the source text as accurately as possible.

Unlike other special-purpose texts, the meaning of legal texts is usually dependent on local context, which is synonymous with legal context. It is in legal system that the texts are to be interpreted rather than the language itself. Contracts, for example, are interpreted according to the law governing the contract regardless of the language in which they are written. Accordingly, if a contract is governed by American law, the translation version of that contract will be interpreted according to American law. If a contract contains elements of foreign law, those elements may be interpreted according to foreign law in some cases.

Since the meaning of legal texts is determined mainly by legal context, lawyers admit that the presumption of the equal meaning can rarely be achieved in practice. Therefore, the main goal of legal translation cannot be to produce a text with the same meaning as the source text. Sarcevic (1997: 55) regards legal translation as "an act of communication in the mechanism of the law" instead of "a process of linguistic transcoding." Hence, the source texts and the target texts must have the same communicative function. This brings us to the second presumption of the legal translation: the presumption of equal effects. Thus, legal translators' main task is to produce a text that will lead to the same legal effects in practice. To produce such a text, legal translators must be able to "understand not only what the words mean and what a sentence mean, but also what legal effect it is supposed to have, and how to achieve that legal effect in the other language"(Schroth 1986: 55-56).

In a word, the goal of legal translation can be defined as to produce a text that is equal in meaning and effect with the source texts, whereby the main emphasis is on effect. That is to say, the target texts will be interpreted and applied by the courts in the same manner as the source texts. This is known as uniform interpretation and application. (Sarcevic 1997: 72) To this end, legal translators must produce a text that has the same communicative function as the source text. This is undoubtedly the most serious matter to be considered by legal translators in their decision-making process.

Chapter Three

Legal English

As the process of translation is always carried out from one language, called the source language, into another, known as the target language, English is cited in most instances when we examine legal translation. There are two grounds justifying the choice of English: the first one is that English is now the dominant language used in the drafting of most legal texts and documents in international organizations and also in bilateral agreements. The second justification is that English is the language that conveys one of the two most important legal cultures in the world, namely, the Anglo-American legal culture and the continental legal culture.

Legal English is the style of English used by lawyers, judges and other legal professionals in the course of their work. It is based on ordinary English but used for specific purposes. Namely, legal English is a variety of English. The development of legal English was strongly influenced by two languages: Latin and French. All of this is still in evidence today: the characteristics of modern legal English are basically explained by the country's legal and linguistic history—a highly unique history.

Chapter Three   Legal English

History of Legal English[1]

Every language is a product of its history, and more specifically, a product of the history of the people who speak it. Legal language is not just a product of the society or jurisdiction in which it is used, but also of the legal profession that speaks and writes it. Legal English is a good example. Its story involves Anglo-Saxon mercenaries, Latin-speaking missionaries, Scandinavian raiders, and Norman invaders, all of whom left their mark not only on England, but on its language.

Legal English was therefore heavily influenced by the forces that shaped the English nation in general. But, in addition, it was formed by the distinct experiences of the profession. The discussion that follows is based on Baker (1990), Mellinkoff (1990) and Tiersma (1999).

The Anglo-Saxon Period

The English language can be said to have begun around 450 A.D., when boatloads of Angles, Jutes, Saxons and Frisians arrived from the Continent. These Germanic invaders spoke closely related languages, which came to form what we call Anglo-Saxon or Old English. Although the Anglo-Saxons seem to have had no distinct legal profession, they did develop a type of legal language, remnants of which have survived until today. Examples include words like *bequeath, goods, guilt, manslaughter, murder, oath, right, sheriff, steal, swear, theft, thief, ward, witness* and *writ*.

Because at this time the Anglo-Saxons were illiterate (except for the very limited use of a runic alphabet), they needed mnemonic devices to help them remember the law. The most common of such devices were rhyme and alliteration, and we find remnants of each in today's legal language. One alliterative phrase

---

[1] This part is a rewritten version of *The Nature of Language* by Peter Tiersma.

that has survived is *to have and to hold*, which is still found in many deeds and also in wedding vows. Numerous modern wills contain the phrase *rest, residue and remainder*, and contracts often have a *hold harmless* clause. An example of rhyme is the maxim, *finders keepers, losers weepers*, which is a well-known albeit not always correct statement of the law.

The Anglo-Saxons used not only Old English as a legal language, but also Latin. Although Latin was originally introduced to England during the Roman occupation of Britain, it became a major force only after the arrival of Christian missionaries in 597. Before long, Latin was the language not only of the church, but of education and learning. The association between literacy and the church became so strong that the two were almost synonymous. The terms *clerk* (someone who can write) and *cleric* or *clergy* (priest) derive from the same Latin root. For centuries, English courts recognized a type of immunity for members of the clergy, who were identified by their ability to read.

The introduction of literacy resulted in many legal transactions being memorialized, or performed, in writing. Several of the early Anglo-Saxon kings created written codes of law, for example. In addition, although writing was seldom essential in this period, dozens of early English written wills and deeds survive. Some of these documents are in Latin, but a substantial number are in Old English.

Not too terribly long after they had themselves invaded England, the Anglo-Saxons found themselves under attack from another group of Germanic warriors: the Vikings. Eventually, a large group of Vikings settled in England and gradually assimilated to the existing population. They ended up speaking English, but in the process they influenced the language by giving it a fair amount of Scandinavian vocabulary. In the legal sphere, their legacy includes the most important legal word in the English language: the word *law* itself. Law derives from the Norse word for "lay" and thus means "that which is laid down."

Chapter Three Legal English

The Norman Conquest and the Introduction of French

The next foreign invasion, the Norman Conquest, had a far more profound and lasting impact on the language of English lawyers. The Normans were originally Vikings who conquered the region of Normandy during the ninth and tenth centuries. In the course of a few generations, these Vikings became French both culturally and linguistically; the Northman had become Normans. William, Duke of Normandy, claimed the English throne and conquered England in 1066. Before long, the English-speaking ruling class was largely supplanted by one that spoke Norman French.

The Normans were accustomed to writing legal documents in Latin, not French. So, the role of Latin expanded. At the same time, English was regarded as the language of a conquered people, and for several hundred years largely faded away as a legal language.

Latin remained important for legal purposes until the early part of the eighteenth century. It was used almost exclusively as the language of court records. The practice of using Latin *versus* in case names harks back to these times. English lawyers and judges were also prone to express sayings or maxims about the law in Latin. At one time, there were many hundreds of maxims about the law, virtually all of them in Latin. Just about all that has survived of Latin in the legal sphere is a small number of these maxims, such as *caveat emptor*, which has infiltrated into general knowledge, and a few sayings regarding general principles of law and legal interpretation, including *de minimis non curat lex* and *expressio unius est exclusio alterius*.

The first century or two following the Norman Conquest saw very little written legislative activity, and to the extent there was any, it was done in Latin. But starting with the thirteenth century, the volume of legislation (as well as other legal documentation) started to increase dramatically. (Clanchy 1993) Latin was still widely used for legal purposes, of course. But around 1275, statutes in French

began to appear. By 1310 almost all acts of Parliament were in that language. During this same time, royal courts were established and judges were appointed who began to dispense justice. Clerics, who had previously done most legal work, were forbidden by the church to do so, and thereafter a distinct profession of lawyers arose. The professional language of these legal professionals was Anglo-French.

Oddly, the use of French in the English legal system grew at the very time that its decline as a living language in England was well under way. Baker (1990) has observed that outside the legal sphere, Anglo-French was in steady decline after 1300. Even the royal household, the last bastion of French, switched to English by the early 1400s. Yet lawyers clung to French as their professional language for another century or two.

Unhappiness about this state of affairs led to what might be considered the first plain English law. In 1362 Parliament enacted the Statute of Pleading, condemning French as "unknown in the said Realm" and lamenting that parties in a lawsuit "have no Knowledge nor Understanding of that which is said for them or against them by their Serjeants and other Pleaders." The statute required that henceforth all pleas be "pleaded, shewed, defended, answered, debated, and judged in the English Tongue." Ironically, the statute itself was in French!

The legal profession seems to have largely ignored this statute. Acts of Parliament did finally switch to English around 1480, but legal treatises and reports of courts cases remained mostly in French throughout the sixteenth century and the first half of the seventeenth. Complaints continued to mount. When the Puritans took over Parliament and abolished the monarchy, they passed a law in 1650 that required all case reports and books of law to be "in the English Tongue only." But when the monarchy was restored, lawyers were once again free to use French, although by then their French was severely degraded.

French had a strong impact on many aspects of modern English, especially in terms of vocabulary. But because it was the main language of the profession for so many centuries, and especially during its formative period, its influence on legal language has been that much greater. For example, just about all the basic terminology for courts and court proceedings is French in origin, including *appeal, attorney, bailiff, bar, claim, complaint, counsel, court, defendant, demurrer, evidence, indictment, judge, judgment, jury, justice, party, plaintiff, plea, plead, sentence, sue, suit, summon, verdict* and *voir dire.*

French influence can also be seen in the substantial number of legal phrases consisting of adjectives following the noun that they modify, which is the usual French word order. Several such combinations are still common in legal English, including *attorney general, court martial, fee simple absolute, letters testamentary, malice aforethought*, and *solicitor general*. Also, Law French allowed the creation of worlds ending in *-ee* to indicate the person who was the recipient or object of an action (*lessee*: "the person leased to"). Lawyers, even today, are coining new words on this pattern, including *asylee, condemnee, detainee, expellee,* and *tippee.*

Legal Language in the New World

The English colonies in the Americas, which later became the United States, were largely populated by people from Britain who were familiar with English law and its idiom. Not surprisingly, perhaps, when the colonies became independent, they retained not only the common law, but its language as well. It should be pointed out that by the time of the American revolution, Latin and French were no longer used as legal languages in England, although they both left behind vestiges (mostly words and maxims) testifying to their earlier dominance. Thus, neither Latin nor French was ever used by the profession in the New World. What the early Americans inherited, or adopted, was legal English, which in the words of Thomas Jefferson was characterized by verbosity, endless tautologies, and "multiplied efforts at certainty by saids and aforesaids." Jefferson and the other founders of the United States might have taken the opportunity to revolutionize not just the judicial system of their young country, but its language as well. But although the

revolutionaries had a negative view of much British legislation, they viewed the common law in a more positive light. And because the common law was expressed in traditional legalese, the adoption of common-law principles almost inevitably entailed the adoption of the language used to express them.

Lexical Features of Legal English

Legal English is characterized by its precision and formality, which are manifested at different levels of legal documents, say at lexical and syntactical levels. This part is devoted to elaborating on the lexical characteristics of legal English, which also gives expression to the historical features of legal English.

Formal Words

First and foremost, legal English is a normative language. The normativeness derives from the fact that law has the basic function of guiding human behavior and regulating human relations in society. In the words of Olivecrona (1962: 177, quoted by Jackson 1985: 315), "…the purpose of all legal enactments, judicial pronouncements, contracts, and other legal acts is to influence men's behavior and direct them in certain ways, thus, the legal language must be viewed primarily as a means to this end." Consequently, the language used in law to achieve its purpose is predominantly prescriptive, directive and imperative.

In legal texts, the solemn and authoritative properties are reflected in the use of a large number of formal words that are seldom used in daily life. For example, American lawyers always speak of *advising* a client when they are merely *telling* him or her something; judges usually write of trials *commencing* and *terminating* rather than simply *beginning* and *ending*. As another example,

§2-209 (2) A signed agreement which excludes modification or rescission

Chapter Three   Legal English

except by a signed writing cannot be otherwise modified or rescinded, but except as between merchants such a requirement on a form supplied by the merchant must be separately signed by the other party. (*Uniform Commercial Code*)

In the above clause, formal words such as "modification" and "rescission" are employed instead of their synonyms "alteration" "cancellation" and suchlike everyday vocabulary. Clearly, the purpose is to impress the general public and to inspire respect for the law.

Legal Terminology and Common Words with Legal Meanings

Legal English is a technical language and legal translation is technical translation involving special language texts. The most obvious way in which legal English differs from ordinary English is its tremendous amount of technical vocabulary. The introduction to the seventh edition of *Black's Law Dictionary* states that it contains approximately 30, 000 entries. In general, the technical vocabulary is divided into two categories: legal terminology and common words with legal meanings.

Legal terminology refers to certain words or phrases with a specific meaning used in the field of law or the profession of law. As one of the most notable features of legal English, they are fixed and stable in meaning. Each terminology usually defines but one given legal concept, and can not be substituted by any other word. (Xiao 2001: 44) Some legal terminologies are shown below with explanations (see also *Oxford Dictionary of Law*):

> *claimant*: a person applying for relief against another person in an action, suit, petition, or any other form of court proceeding. (Before the introduction of the Civil Procedure Rules in 1999, a claimant was called a *plaintiff*.)
>
> *defendant*: a person against whom court proceedings are brought
>
> *cause of action*: the facts that entitle a person to sue

burden of proof: the duty of a party to litigation to prove a fact or facts in issue

These terminologies are endowed with a single and definite meaning which only appears in the contexts of law. Using legal terminology is an effective way employed by lawmakers to achieve accuracy.

Although much of the vocabulary is quite distinctively legal, there are also many words that have both an ordinary and legal meaning. Tiersma (1999:111-112) has named these words "Legal Homonyms," i.e., words that share the same form, but differ completely in meaning from those in ordinary English. This can sometimes be confusing for nonspecialists who might think that they understand a word or phrase while in fact they do not. For instance, when a lawyer tells someone that she is going to *file a complaint* against him, it does not mean that she plans merely to make a complaint, but that she plans to initiate a lawsuit against him.

To make a clear comparison between the ordinary meaning and legal meaning of common words, some words are picked out in the following table. The ordinary meanings are taken from *Longman Dictionary of Contemporary English Language & Culture* (2004) and the legal ones from *Black's Law Dictionary* (2004).

Words	Ordinary Meanings	Legal Meanings
action	the fact or process of doing things	a lawsuit (either civil or criminal)
counterpart	a person or thing that has the same purpose or does the same job as another in a different system	duplicate of a document
demise	death	to lease
hand	either of the movable parts at the end of a person's arm, including the fingers	signature

（续表）

Words	Ordinary Meanings	Legal Meanings
party	an occasion when people meet together to enjoy themselves; a group of people doing something together	a litigant in law suit

Words and Phrases from Old and Middle English, Latin and Old French

Legal English is mixed in a particularly striking way as a language of interaction between Old and Middle English, Latin and Old French. These languages left a deep imprint on legal English—an imprint that remain clearly visible. Often, Latin and French expressions form part of the most basic vocabulary of English law. Some of these express the very foundations of English legal thinking.

Archaic Words from Old English and Middle English

When analyzing the development of the English language, we can roughly divide the process into three periods: Old English or Anglo-Saxon Period (AD 450—AD 1100), Middle English Period (AD 1100—AD 1500), and Modern English Period (after AD 1500). The reason for this division of the period of English development is that the language experienced extraordinary changes during each period.

It goes without saying that the English used today is attached to the Old and Middle English to a large extent. However, it is also obvious that the changes of the English have caused numerous Old and Middle English words and meanings to fade out of the everyday use. In legal English, however, quite a large number of archaic words survived the evolution of the English language. A special case of archaisms is the persistence in legal English of compound adverbs based on

the simple deictics "here" "there" "where" and so on, often referring to the text or document in which they appear or to one under discussion. (Alcaraz & Hughes 2008: 9) Some words of this kind are given bellow:

Example

here-	there-
hereafter	thereafter
hereby	thereby
herein	therein
hereto	thereto

These words listed above are completely out-of-date to modern English users. Although they are not difficult to understand in terms of meaning, they are exceptionally strange and unacceptable to those who have rare access to legal documents. Therefore, it is not inappropriate to say that the existence of these archaic words, to some extent, defamiliarize the non-lawyers from the language of the law. From the perspective of history, this is no coincidence for the survival of the archaic words in legal English.

Further analysis mainly goes to some of the historical factors, such as the development of the law and the Plain English Movement. In his book *The Language of the Law*, Mellinkoff (1990) holds that the word "law" itself is of Scandinavian origin. The word "law" has a long history behind it, so does the common law in Britain. The British Isles witnessed the Celtic invasion, the Roman occupation, the Anglo-Saxon invasion, the Norman Conquest and the establishment of the modern Britain, throughout which the common law gradually took shape. In spite of the great historical upheavals, the law never loses its status in British history and remains a favorite tool of the ruling class to govern the masses. To maintain its functions, the law is inclined to be stable. When the time came that it is a must to change an existing law, it is on more occasions through modification or amendment rather than radical change. As a result, using antiquated terminology bestows a sense of timelessness on the legal system, as something that has lasted through the centuries and is therefore deserving great respect. (Tiersma 1999: 95-97) In other words, archaic words help to ensure the stiffness and formality of the legal English, and meanwhile make people think that the law has a long tradition and can't be changed easily. Hence, the language of the law has also displayed the feature of inheritance and consistency.

Whenever the archaic words in legal English are touched, the Plain English Movement should never be left out. Just as the name suggests, the Plain English Movement, starting in the 1970s, is a social movement, which advocates writing straightforwardly. The premise behind the Plain English Movement is that legal documents ought to be plainer and more comprehensible to the average people. Many absurdities of traditional legalese are pointed out in Mellinkoff's book, *The Language of the Law* (1990). The Movement spurs, to some extent, the development of legal English towards plainer English. It has abolished some time-honored legal terms for modern equivalents. A "subpoena" is now a "witness summons," an "in camera hearing" is now a "private hearing," and a "writ" is now a "claim form." However, due to the function of the archaic words in terms of style, it is rather difficult or even impossible to go deep into the simplification of the legal language for it should not proceed at the sacrifice of the precision and economy of the language of the law.

Words and Phrases from Latin

It goes without saying that English, as a cosmopolitan language, borrowed a large amount of words from many other languages. More than half of English words can trace back to their Latin origin. As early as AD 597, when Christianity was introduced to Britain, the Latin language started to exert its influence on the English language. There are mainly two ways for Latin to be coined into English. Some Latin words entered into French before entering into English; others entered

into English directly.

Latin is in evidence everywhere in legal English. This was partly decided by the tradition of the Common law system. Originally, legal Latin came from Roman law, and the Common Law system is greatly influenced by the Roman Law system, which can best be proved by the fact that sometimes it is taken as an equivalent of the Roman Law system by modern jurists. After AD 1066—the time of Norman Conquest—Latin took the place of English as the dominant written language of English law. At the beginning of modern times, court judgments were generally drawn up in Latin. The same language was also used in legal dealings. Even after Latin was abandoned in its capacity of legal language, legal documents were still long peppered with a large number of Latin words.

Nowadays, Latin is still quite in evidence in legal documents of the common law system. Many words in legal English have Latin origins, e.g., *alibi* (in a criminal case, a defense that the accused was somewhere else when the crime was committed), *pro forma* (for the sake of form, as a matter of form), *de facto* (in fact), *contra legem* (against the law) and *force majeure* (irresistible force or compulsion such as will excuse a party from performing his or her part of a contract). The following passage is a case in point to illustrate the importance of Latin in legal English.

Abinitio it should be said that there is a good **prima facie** case for the decision of Lord Irvine, the Lord High Chancellor, to simplify the language used in court as part of the civil law reforms which bear the **imprimatur** of the Master of the Rolls, Lord Woolf. From April 26 (1999) Lord Irvine wants lawyers, **pro bono publico**, to be much more straightforward in the way they speak **pendente lite**. Out will go, **inter alia**, hearings **in camera** or **ex parte**. In will come hearings in private or without notice. Plaintiffs will be replaced by claimants. Newspaper editors will no longer live in terror of writs. Instead they will tremble at claim forms. Mr. Anton Piller will soon be forgotten except in cobwebbed old tomes. The eponymous legal term will be succeeded, **ad infinitum** and **sine die** by a plain old search order.

The passage above is a judgment offered by Ma (Ma 2009:52). Ten Latin words, which are bold and underlined, should appear in this passage of 145 words. Maybe this is only a coincidence for this passage to be so densely dotted with Latin words. However, it is still a somewhat solid proof of the importance of Latin in legal English. As time goes by, plus the influence of the Plain English Movement, many Latin words are not in active use nowadays, but it is still an important footprint in the history of legal English.

Words from Old French

English also borrowed a great many French words, which is especially prominent in legal English. The reason why French could exert such a great impact on legal English is that it had close contact with English in history.

The Norman Conquest in the year AD 1066 brought about, for the first time, the unification of the law in Britain. It was from that time that the early form of Common Law began to take shape. Due to the fact that Normans, the ruling class, spoke French, French naturally became the official language of Britain and was widely used in courts and schools.

As is well known, among the many forces that shaped English language, the French influence after the Norman Conquest was paramount. As a result, thousands of English words are Old French or Norman in origin, and the rules of word-formation have been profoundly marked by this contact. First of all, most of the technical vocabulary of legal English goes back to Old French (as to meaning, the [roughly] equivalent word in modern legal French often has another root, as seen in the translations below). A list of examples could go on almost endlessly, e.g., agreement (Fr. accord, convention, contrat), arrest (Fr. garde à vue), assault (Fr. assaut), crime (Fr. infraction), damage (Fr. dommage), felony (Fr. crime, infraction majeure), heir (Fr. héritier), misdemeanor (Fr. contravention, délit mineur), trespass

(Fr. transgression, intrusion). As for administration, examples include authority (Fr. autorité), chancellor (Fr. chancelier). In matters of the legal process, vocabulary of French origin is very strongly in evidence: action (Fr. action), appeal (Fr. recours), attorney (Fr. avocat), bailiff (Fr. huissier), bar (Fr. barreau), complaint (Fr. plainte, réclamation, demande introductive d'instance), counsel (Fr. avocat, conseil, conseiller), defendant (Fr. défendeur), judge (Fr. juge), jury (Fr. jury), party (Fr. partie), plaintiff (Fr. demandeur), process (Fr. procès), sentence (Fr. jugement, condamnation, peine), suit (Fr. poursuite, action; affaire), summons (Fr. citation), verdict (Fr. verdict, décision du jury, jugement). Lastly, French strongly influenced the formation of English words. (Tiersma 1999: 30–33) The past participle in Old French was formed by adding to the word stem the letter -*e* or the letters -*ee* (corresponding to the letter -é in Modern French). French used this ending to denote, for example, the person obtaining something or forming the object of an action, e.g., acquittee, arrestee, condemnee. Correspondingly, a word denoting an active person (the doer) was given the ending -or. In this way, opposite positions were created: employer/employee, trustor/trustee, mortgagor/mortgagee, vendor/vendee. On the other hand, a feature typical of legal English, dating back to the time of law French, is that the adjective is often placed after the noun in petrified phrases, e.g., *accounts payable, attorney general, court martial, letters patent* and so on.

Emergence of New Legal Terms

In spite of the reputation that legal English is stiff and conservative, it can actually be quite innovative and creative at times. Of course, lawyers and judges are unlikely to adopt a new term when the concept to which an existing term refers is still part of current law. Nevertheless, as both natural and social sciences have advanced by leaps and bounds since the 19th century, new products, techniques and ideas have emerged endlessly, so have the new legal terms, such as *computer crime, smuggling of drugs, securities act* etc. (Xiao 2001: 45) For example, the

Chapter Three Legal English

development of electronic commerce on the Internet has resulted in the coinage of many new legal terms, including terminology for types of licenses that can currently be created online (Tiersma 2008: 16-17):

– shrinkwrap licenses (where the purchaser assents to terms contained in boxed software or in a user's manual by opening the box);

– clickwrap licenses (where a purchaser clicks on a box or icon on a website, thereby manifesting assent to the terms of the license);

– browsewrap licenses (where a purchaser on the Internet clicks on a notice that takes him to a separate web page containing the full text of the license agreement).

There are also many words that have been coined for electronic transactions by prefixing an *e-* (on the analogy of email), such as *e-commerce*, *e-contracts*, *e-discovery*, *e-signature* and so on.

Words and Phrases for Precision and Fuzziness

Precision has long been considered as the soul and vitality of legal language, which is determined by its prescriptive nature. A minor mistake in the statements of legal texts would cause serious problems, losses and disputes. As a result, lawmakers, lawyers, and judges are always careful and cautious to select the words to describe legal content as accurate as possible. There are a number of features that have the capacity to increase the precision of legal texts. (Tiersma 2008: 21) At lexical level, one is the use of lists of synonyms or near-synonyms. Although sometimes such lists are completely redundant as we may see on other occasions, they can be helpful in specifying exactly what is meant. When studying the legal texts attentively, we can easily find a mountain of lists of synonymous words, say, *terms and conditions, rights and interests, losses and damages, sign and issue, null and void, rules, requirements, and regulations, terminate, cancel or revoke* etc. In these phrases, the second or the third word is often used to reaffirm and

complement the first one to make the language of law more precise and complete.

Another example is that the careful repetition of words can sometimes be useful. A pronoun is rarely used unless there is no possibility of confusion. If a statute refers to a *city*, the term should be used consistently, rather than using *town* or *municipality* in the same meaning, nor will the pronoun *it* be used. In short, law demands precision and exactness. The drafters and translators of legal texts must spare no efforts to ensure that a text says exactly what it is meant to say, and leave no space for misinterpretation.

Though precision is the most prominent feature of legal language, fuzzy words and expressions are inevitable in legal language. Just as Gibbons (2003: 38) puts, precision is not extremely clarity; it may also involve selecting the appropriate level of fuzziness of flexibility. On one hand, language is inherently fuzzy. Most often, people tend to think that anything that can be said can be said clearly, and anything that can be thought can be thought clearly. In actual use, language falls far short of such as ideal conception. Moreover and importantly, the universe and human behavior are inherently uncertain and indeterminate and people are not able to foresee every possible future contingency. Law attempts to cover every situation which might arise in the enforcement of statute and tries to cover unforeseen situation which might appear in human society. (Dong 2004: 60-61) The use of fuzziness enhances the foreseeability, applicability and flexibility of legislations.

Legal English is full of imprecise words and impressions. English legal terms such as *fair and reasonable*, *due care,* and *due process of law* are fuzzy and elusive. So are the abstract legal expressions such as *justice*, *due diligence*, and *reasonable endeavours*. As said before, linguistic uncertainty is inherent in language, and cannot be eliminated. Take *Article 4 in Libel Act* for example,

(1) … for <u>any term not exceeding two years</u>, and to <u>pay such fine as court shall award</u>.

(2) The phrase "place of residence" shall include the street, square, or

place where the person to whom it refers shall reside…(*quoted by* Du 2001: 307)

In the above two examples, the underlined expressions are fuzzy in meanings. Example (1) doesn't specify the definite *time* or the exact amount of *fine*, and example (2) doesn't give an accurate definition of *place*. In this way, the use of fuzzy expressions enhances the flexibility to cover future contingency, and also give greater discretion to those charged with implementing a law.

Hence, precision and fuzziness are not contradictory to each other but complementary, which are unitary facets of legal English.

Syntactic Features of Legal English

Legal English has been considered a kind of Language for Specific Purposes (LSP), sometimes even a foreign language by some, which is not only because of the legal jargons and technical words embedded in legal English but also for its syntax with special characteristics.

Declarative Sentences

English sentences can be classified into four categories in line with their purposes: declarative sentence (to make a statement), interrogative sentence (to request information), exclamative sentence (to express emotion), imperative sentence (to give a command).

Legal texts are basically associated with the authorization of rights, imposition of obligations or punishment, and enforcement of law. Everything should be based on actual facts without any subjective wills or personal emotions. As a result, the use of declarative sentences is predominant in English legal texts with the exclusion of the other three types of sentences. (Xiao 2000: 49) For example,

(1) A contract for sale of goods may be made in any manner sufficient to show agreement, including conduct by both parties which recognizes the existence of such a contract.

(2) An agreement sufficient to constitute a contract for sale may be found even though the moment of its making is undetermined.

(3) Even though one or more terms are left open a contract for sale does not fail for indefiniteness if the parties have intended to make a contract and there is a reasonably certain basis for giving an appropriate remedy.

Quoted from the *Uniform Commercial Code*, the above three sentences are all declarative sentences, stipulating the basic requirements of forming a contract. In this way, people can have a clear idea of law provisions.

Long Sentences

The most distinguished feature of legal English is that it is peppered with unusually long and complex sentences. Although long sentences are also in frequent use in scientific English and business English, they are much more prominent in legal English in terms of frequency and range. As illustrated in *Introduction to English Stylistics*, the length of the English sentences in legal texts is far longer than that of ordinary English sentences—17 words in one sentence. (Wang & Ding 1987: 287) This preference for long sentences is due to the need for covering all possible conditions and contingencies of a particular issue, as short ones may result in ambiguity in the interpretation of legal texts. Various attributive and adverbial clauses, prepositional phrases and nonfinite forms of verb are interwoven with each other for the sake of clarity and preciseness. One section of the *British Drug Trafficking Act* is a single highly complex sentence of over 250 words in length. (Alcaraz & Hughes 2008) They hold that it is typical of the syntax of British statutes both in length and in the complexity of its layout, with multiple subordination and post-modifiers. The example given below, which can act as a lively demonstration of this feature, is taken from *Federal Civil Judicial Procedure and Rules*.

> Art. 994 (c) The commission in establishing categories of offences for use in the guidelines and policy statements governing the imposition of sentences of probation, a fine, or imprisonment, governing the imposition of other authorize sanctions, governing the size of a fine or the length of a term of probation, imprisonment, or supervise release, and governing the conditions of probation, supervised release, or imprisonment, shall consider whether the following matters among others have any relevance to the nature, extent, place of service, or other incidents of an appropriate sentence and shall take them into account only to the extent that they do have relevance—the grade of the offense; the circumstances under which the offense was committed which mitigate or aggravate the seriousness of the offense; the nature and degree of the harm caused by the offense, including whether it involved property, irreplaceable property, a person, a number of persons, or a breach of public trust; the community view of the gravity of the offense; the public concern generated by the offense; the deterrent effect a particular sentence may have on the commission of the offense by others; and the current incidence of the offense in the community and in the Nation as a whole. (*Federal Civil Judicial Procedure and Rules*, 1996)

The sentence above is an unconventionally long one of 200 words, with multiple post-modifiers, such as "governing the imposition of sentences of probation, a fine, or imprisonment," "governing the imposition of other authorized sanctions" and so on. The reason for this syntactic feature of legal English goes to the functions of legal English in history.

Passive Sentences

Stylistically, legal English tends to be relatively impersonal. The abundant use of passive sentences is one of the most common methods of promoting the impersonal style. Probably the principal reason is that impersonal expressions create the impression that law is objective and not a respecter of persons. It also is related to abstractness, which is essential for the expression of general and broad legal principles. (Matilla 2006: 51, 73–74) It is undoubtedly true that one common effect of the passive mood is to suppress the identity of the agent responsible for the performance of the act. For instance, the sentence "The contract was breached" simply states the fact. It doesn't indicate who the wrongdoer was or who breached the contract. This can also be seen from the following example in which the passive voice has been underlined.

Where an action <u>has been instituted</u> in a court competent under paragraph 1 or 2 of this article or where judgment <u>has been delivered</u> by such a court, no new action may <u>be started</u> between the same parties on the same grounds unless the judgment of the court before which the first action <u>was instituted</u> is not enforceable in the country in which the new proceedings <u>are instituted</u>. (*United Nations Convention on the Carriage of Goods by Sea, 1978, Part V. Article 21, 4(a)*)

Within target-language norms, it is usually easy to preserve the equivalent effect in translation, thus keeping the stress on the action, rule or decision rather than on the personality of the doer. Nevertheless, the Security Exchange Commission (SEC) is one example of an official body that is sensitive to the appearance of obscurity that over-use of the passive can convey. A good example of how clarity can be achieved by the switch from passive to active, and from impersonal to personal (second person address directed at the reader) is provided by the following case of rewriting of one of the sentences in a prospectus.

(Old version): No person has been authorized to give any information or make any representation other than those contained or incorporated by reference in this joint proxy statement/prospectus, and, if given or made, such information or representation must not be relied upon as having been authorized.

(New version): You should rely only on the information contained in this document or that we have referred you to. We have not authorized anyone to provide you with information that is different.

Conditionals and Hypothetical Formulations

Legal English is full of conditionals and hypothetical formulations. In texts like statutes, contracts and handbooks containing procedural rules, many possible situations, factual scenarios and exceptions must be provided for. Generally, the legal statements contain three essential elements: condition, legal subject and legal action. The former one is used to describe the fact-situation, and the latter two are used to prescribe the statement of law. If we use X to stand for condition, Y for legal subject, Z for legal action, most legal statements can develop into a fixed formula: "If X, then Y shall do Z" or "If X, then Y shall be Z." Although most conditionals are led by the word "if," legal language is unusually rich in syntactic indicators of condition and hypothesis, which may be positive (e.g. "when" "where" "assuming that" and so on) or negative (e.g., "unless" "failing" "except as/where/if" "but for" and so on). More often than not, legal documents mix positive with negative conditions and hypotheses. The following passage is a typical example of this kind:

Where either party fails to perform their side of the bargain, then, *subject to clause 15* above, *if notice of non-performance is given* in writing by the injured party within seven days, or, *in the event that communication is impossible* until the ship reaches a port of call, as soon thereafter as is

practically possible, the injured party shall be entitled to treat the contract as discharged *except as otherwise provided* in this contract. (Alcaraz & Hughes 2008)

Use of Logical Connectors and Modifiers

If, after the signing of the Agreement, the Chinese government either at the State, provincial, municipal or local level adopts any new law, regulation, decree or rule, amends or repeals any provision of any law, regulation, decree or rule, or adopts any different interpretation or method of implementation of any law, regulation, decree or rule, which contravenes this Agreement or which materially and adversely affects a Party's economic benefit under this Agreement, then upon written notice thereof from the affected party to the other Party, the Parties shall promptly consult and decide whether (i) to continue to implement this Agreement in accordance with the original provisions thereof as per the relevant provisions of the *Contract Law of the People's Republic of China*; or (ii) to effectuate necessary adjustments in order to preserve each Party's economic benefit under this Agreement on a basis no less favourable than the economic benefit it would have received if such law, regulation, decree or rule had not been adopted, amended, replaced or so interpreted or implemented. (Sun 2003: 5)

This provision of the Agreement is made up of a coherent and well-organized sentence with 171 words, including a conditional, logical connectors and a large number of modifiers, which are to be discussed separately (except the conditional that was analyzed above).

Logical connectors *and/or* is particularly important in expressing the intended logical relations correctly in legal texts. As in general English, the connector *and* is conjunctive, whereas *or* is disjunctive. In legal texts, these connectors may be decisive in determining whether a person has broken the law, whether a contracting party has fulfilled its obligations and so forth. For instance, the conditions specified in the above Agreement "adopts any new law, regulation, decree or rule, amends," "repeals any provision of any law, regulation, decree or rule," "adopts any different interpretation or method of implementation of any law, regulation, decree or rule" are connected by *or*, this signifies that these stipulated conditions are to be applied alternatively rather than cumulatively.

Besides, modifiers also play an important part of the constructing the lengthy sentences in legal texts. The modifiers in the above Agreement are listed as follows:

Adverbial of time: after the signing of the Agreement

Attributive clause: which contravenes this Agreement or which materially and adversely affects a Party's economic benefit under this Agreement

Adverbial of manner: in accordance with the original provisions thereof as per the relevant provisions of the *Contract Law of the People's Republic of China*

on a basis no less favorable than the economic benefit it would have received if such law, regulation, decree or rule had not been adopted, amended, replaced or so interpreted or implemented

Adverbial of purpose: in order to preserve each Party's economic benefit under this Agreement

These modifiers are inserted at appropriate syntactic positions functioning as internal modifications and restrictions within the sentences. The density of subordination and parenthetic restriction is particularly frequent in the texts of laws and of contracts, and gives them characteristic air of complexity. (Bhatia 1993: 116) The following are among the common conjunctions and prepositional phrases of this type found in legal English: "notwithstanding" "under" "subject to" "having regard to" " relating to" "on" "pursuant to" "in order to" "in accordance with" and so on.

Chapter Four

Legal Translation and Equivalence

Legal translation is not mere a stylized transfer, but regarded as "an act of communication in the mechanism of the law" (Sarcevic 1997: 55). Unlike mathematics or chemistry where there is an objective extra-linguistic reference, legal realities are conceived as the result of legal discourse which creates its own reality from different historic traditions in different languages, and which cannot coincide in the concepts of analysis or can only coincide partially when they focus on a common international legal phenomenon. (Anderson 1987: 67)

Many specialists have held that the main purpose of translation is the search for equivalence, that is, finding an equivalent expression in the target language for the words or sentences coming from the source language. The term "equivalence" is thus central in translation theory, since the finding of an equal or similar expression in the target language is not always attainable. The questions of equivalence are especially problematic in the field of legal translation. The great challenge that legal translators may encounter is the transfer of legal concepts among different legal systems rather than simple inter-lingual transfer. As a result, legal translators must take account of the communicative function of the legal texts and the elements constituting the socio-cultural situation in which it is produced.

Chapter Four   Legal Translation and Equivalence

Factors Influencing Legal Translation

It is a fact that with growing experience of translation, the transfer of words, sentences and texts from one language to another is anything but mechanical work. Finding the meaning of legal texts is often not easy, even when one is working entirely within a familiar legal system and with a language acquired as his mother tongue, let alone to translate them into another language with equivalent authenticity. The nature of legal language contributes to the complexity and difficulty in legal translation. This is compounded by further complications arising from social and cultural factors. Specifically, the factors influencing legal translation include cultural discrepancies, incongruence of legal systems, and linguistic non-equivalence. All of these are closely related and interwoven.

Cultural Discrepancies

Legal context serves only a starting point for the translation of legal texts, and the pragmatic considerations should also be taken into account. Language and culture or social context are closely integrated and interdependent. Snell-Hornby (1988: 42) argues that, in translation, language should not be seen as an isolated phenomenon suspended in a vacuum but as an integral part of culture, and the text is embedded in a given situation, which is itself conditioned by its socio-cultural background. Law is an expression of the culture, and it is expressed through legal language. Legal language, like other language use, is a social practice and legal texts necessarily bear the imprint of such practice or organizational background. (Goodrich 1987: 2) In other words, legal concepts are conceived as the result of legal discourse which creates its own reality from different traditions and cultural backgrounds.

Religion and Tradition

Religion, as a kind of social phenomenon, is an indispensible part of some people's spiritual life. According to different criteria, religions can be classified into different categories, such as Christianity, Catholicism, Buddhism, Taoism, and Islamism. Religious culture plays an important role in cross-cultural communication because it has penetrated into almost every aspect of social life.

The prominent cultural role played by religion can be best demonstrated by its relations with law. In the ancient times, religion was closely related to morality and law. Some of the classics are typical examples of the combination of religion, morality and law, such as the Koran of Islamism and the Manusmrti of Indian Buddhism. In the Europe of Middle Ages, Christianity and Catholicism, as two religions of great power, maintained an interdependent but competitive relationship with the political regime. At that time the ecclesiastical law and secular existed side by side. In some ancient civilizations, there is something common to their statute law of the early times, i.e., they all had a close kinship with religion. For example, both the Ancient Babylon and the Ancient India had their legislative guiding ideologies based on religious ideas. Nowadays, although political regime has been largely separated from religion and the influence of religion over the legal sphere has also been weakened, the fundamental ideas in religious codes still have a fairly great impact on modern laws. Judging from the historical development of law, religion is an important source of modern law.

Christianity is one of the important sources of western tradition and, to some extent, it forms the basis of western legal tradition. In the history of legal development in the western world, it evolved from Roman law to canon law and finally the Germanic Law. Christianity played an important role in this process. In fact, it greatly supplemented the modern common law system. In the 11th century and 12th century, Christianity and the canon law facilitated the codification of western laws in terms of legal criteria.

Law and religion have always been intertwined with each other throughout

Chapter Four Legal Translation and Equivalence

history. Berman (2003) pointed out in his book *Law and Religion* that there are four elements that are common to law and religion, i.e., ritual, tradition, authority and universality. These four elements determine the close relationship and even the common ground between law and religion. Although the western law and Christianity have also experienced conflicts from time to time, they are highly interdependent on each other. The western law, without Christianity, will be reduced to mechanical doctrinarism; Christianity, without the western law, will be deprived of its social effectiveness.

In modern western laws, Christianity successfully finds a lot of ways to manifest itself. For instance, western people value highly the rights of freedom and equality. This is, in essence, a deviation of the religious doctrine, which believes that everyone is the descendant of God and everyone is born equal. As a result, everyone is protected by law. If the right is born with them, such as the right of existence, it is illegal for anyone or any organization to deprive them of it. As another example, *Holy Bible*, the classic of Christianity, advocated highly the principle of honesty and equality. This principle has successful found way into the western legal tradition, which presents itself in the legal term "good faith."

In western countries, tradition is an important and sometimes the dominant factor shaping the law of the society, as a result of which customary law is recognized as one of the formal sources of law. Anyone who is familiar with the Anglo-American legal system knows *Good Samaritan Laws*. They are laws or acts protecting those who choose to serve and tend to aid others who are injured or ill. The laws are intended to reduce bystanders' hesitation to assist, for fear of being sued or prosecuted for unintentional injury or wrongful death. *Good Samaritan Laws* take their name from a parable told by Jesus commonly referred to as the Parable of the Good Samaritan which is contained in *Luke* 10:25-37. It recounts the aid given by one traveller (from the area known as Samaria) to another traveller of a different religious and ethnic background who had been beaten and robbed by bandits. While translating this phrase, legal translators cannot give an accurate translation if they don't know this parable. As a result, the symbolic and connotational meanings of cultural specific legal concepts cannot be translated easily and thus tend to remain a mystery even when extensive explanations are used. (Sarcevic 1985: 127-133)

Social Context

As a social science, law is a regime of adjusting relations and ordering human behaviors through the force of socially organized group. People usually need to enact specialized laws to solve various real-life problems. A legal text thus has a social meaning that can be understood only by examining the social context in which the text is produced. For instance, *Baby M Laws* came into being in the United States in the 1980s. With the technological development of artificial insemination, many infertile women are searching for a "surrogate mother." It is similar to the practice of " 借腹生子 " in ancient China, but the husband and the surrogate mother do not have any sexual relationship. Usually it's the physician who got the sperm from the husband and inseminated the surrogate mother. After giving birth to the baby, the mother shall give it back to the biological father. Sometimes, the surrogate mother would break the surrogacy contract and refuse to give the baby back, thus causing a lawsuit on fighting for the baby. The custody case of Baby M once created a great sensation in America. Baby M was the pseudonym for the infant named Melissa Stern in the case. Finally, the court invalidated surrogacy contracts as against public policy, but awarded custody of Baby M to the biological father under a "best interest of the child" analysis and gave the surrogate mother visitation rights. Later, others courts invoke this case to judge similar lawsuits, and then formed the case law called "Baby M Laws" (《代理孕母法》). (Zhu 2000: 47）

Examples like this can make a long list. Some legal concepts are direct products of a society's history and culture, such as "yellow dog contract," "old leg," "policy of carrots and stick" and so on. Some fuzzy terms are easily translated but

Chapter Four Legal Translation and Equivalence

are interpreted differently by courts of different jurisdictions, such as "good faith," "the best interests of the child" etc. These would probably frustrate a translator who is not familiar with the western society and culture. Just as Melinkoff (1992: 98) puts, legal language shares with science a concern for coherence and precision; and with culture a respect for social and historical tradition. Legal translators must overcome cultural barriers between source language and target language societies when reproducing a target language version of a law originally written for the source language readers.

Incongruency of Legal Systems

The law of a country or region is certainly influenced by its culture. In fact some legal anthropologists claim that legal studies cannot be separated from culture, i.e., legal culture. Nonetheless, in regard to translation, translators of legal texts are concerned primarily with legal, not cultural transfer. Back in 1974 L.J. Constantmesco, a well-known comparative lawyer, defined legal translation as a double operation consisting of both legal and interlingual transfer.

Due to differences in historical and cultural development, the elements of the source legal system cannot be simply transposed into the target legal system (Sarcevic 1997:13). As a result, the main challenge to the legal translator is the incongruency of legal systems.

Differences in Legal Systems

Roman Jakobson divides translation activity into three categories: intralingual translation, a rewording of signs in one language with signs from the same language; interlingual translation, or the interpretation of signs in one language with signs from another language; and intersemiotic translation, or the transfer of the signs in one language to no-verbal sign system. (Gentzler 2004: 88) Similarly, we may borrow the prefixes "intra-" and "inter-" and divide the translation of legal texts into two types with respect to the involved legal systems: intra-legal-system translation

and inter-legal-system translation. (Li & Zhang 2006:17) The former refers to the translation of legal texts into different languages under the same legal system, while the latter involves two or more legal systems. Legal translation discussed in this book is no doubt the inter-legal-system translation. As a result, it is much more complicated because the source and target legal systems are different. The source text is structured in a way that suits its own legal system; the target text is to be read by someone who is familiar with another legal system and its language. (Mellinkof 1992:88)

As for the classification of world legal systems, the two most influential legal families in the world are the Common Law and the Civil Law families. About 80% of the countries in the world belong to these two systems.

Countries Following Common or Civil Law

The United States of America, Canada, England and Wales, India, New Zealand and Australia are generally considered common law countries. Because they were all once subjects or colonies of Great Britain, they have often retained the tradition of common law. The state of Louisiana in the United States uses bijuridicial civil law because it was once a colony of France.

Civil law countries include all of South America (except Guyana), almost all of Europe (including Germany, France, and Spain), North African countries, Japan and South Korea.

There are also mixed systems of law that derive from more than one legal family. They follow a combination of both the Common Law and the Civil Law, such as South Africa, Louisiana in the US, the Province of Quebec, Scotland, the Philippines and Greece. China's law system may be considered as a hybrid of traditional Chinese Law, the Civil Law and Socialist Law.

Below is a discussion on common vs. civil law systems:

History

The English Common Law system is the legal tradition that evolved in England from the 11th century. Its legal principles appear for the most part in

Chapter Four Legal Translation and Equivalence

reported judgments in relation to specific fact situations arising in disputes that courts have to adjudicate. Thus, the Common Law is predominantly founded on a system of case law or judicial precedent. (Cao 2008:25)

In contrast, the Civil Law originated in ancient Roman Law and was later developed through the Middle Ages by medieval legal scholars. The major sources of its legal norms and rules are organized codes or collections. These are normally divided into a civil code, a penal code, and administrative code, a code of commercial law, and a written constitution that stands above them all as a "law of laws" setting out the basic rights and principles from which all the rest are held to flow. (Alcarza & Hughes 2008: 48)

Legal Representation

In both civil and common law countries, lawyers and judges play an important role.

However, in common law, the judge often acts as a referee, as two lawyers argue their side of the case. Generally, the judge, and sometimes a jury, listens to both sides to come to a conclusion about the case.

In civil law countries, the judge is usually the main investigator, and the lawyer's role is to advise a client on legal proceedings, write legal pleadings, and help provide favorable evidence to the investigative judge.

Constitutions

Though not a rule, common law countries may not always follow a constitution or a code of laws.

In civil law, the constitution is generally based on a code of laws, or codes applying to specific areas, like tax law, corporate law, or administrative law.

Contracts

Freedom of contract is very extensive in common law countries, i.e., very little or no provisions are implied in contracts by law. Civil law countries, on the other hand, have a more sophisticated model for contract with provisions based in the law.

LEGAL TRANSLATION

Precedent

The decisions of judges are always binding in common law countries, although that does not mean the decision may not be appealed. In the United States, for example, cases may be heard by a network of federal or state courts, with the federal Supreme Court holding ultimate power. Generally, the ruling of the last court that a case visits remains the final, binding verdict. That case may later be used as precedent to argue similar cases in the future.

In civil law countries, only the judicial decisions of administrative and constitutional courts are binding outside the original case. In essence, the concept of precedent, i.e., past cases can determine the outcome of future ones, is not used.

Terminological Differences

Legal concepts, legal norms and application of laws differ in each individual society reflecting the differences in that society. As David and Brierley (1985:19) state, each legal system has its own characteristics and,

> ...has a vocabulary used to express concepts, its rules are arranged into categories, it has techniques for expressing rules and interpreting them, it is linked to a view of the social order itself which determines the way in which the law is applied and shapes the very function of law in that society.

It can be shown that the boundaries between the meanings of concepts of different legal systems are incongruent. For example, although etymological equivalents such as *contract* and *contrat* even signify the same object, they are not identical at the conceptual level. The English concept of contract is considerably broader than its French equivalent *contrat*, which is restricted to transactions involving mutuality of agreement and obligation. (Tallon 1990:284-290)

In Britain and America, there are many legal terminologies that are quite distinctive from those of Chinese legal system because of the influence of the native legal traditions. They may not or may only partially correspond to those of Chinese legal system. Take the *burglary* for example, its most common translation is "夜盗罪" or "夜盗行为". Unfortunately, the translation just does the job partly. In common law, *burglary* used to mean an actual breaking into a dwelling at night with intent to commit a felony. However, some statutes have expanded *burglary* to include any unlawful entry into or remaining in a building or vehicle with intent to commit a crime. Time is not limited to the night, and the crime can include theft, inflicting grievous bodily harm, causing criminal damage and rape of a person in the building. It should not just refer to "夜盗罪" 或 "夜盗行为". There is a similar crime in Chinese criminal law named "非法侵入他人住宅罪", which is not equivalent to *burglary* either. The so-called "非法侵入他人住宅罪" means the act of breaking into another person's residence without the host's permission or unreasonably refusing to exit even after the host's request. If the criminal suspect aims to commit the crimes of theft, murder, robbery, rape etc, he will be convicted according to these crimes instead of concurrent punishment. At this point, it is contradictory to *burglary*. Concerning the above factors, it is proper to translate *burglary* into "恶意侵入他人住宅罪".

Despite the differences, it should be noted that the Common Law and the Civil Law families are not incompatible. We should not exaggerate the differences or believe that the translation between them is somehow impossible. There has been convergence due to mutual influence between the two families. However, the incongruency of legal systems is a major source of difficulty in legal translation.

Linguistic Differences

According to Saussure, there are two types of languages: one is the least systematical and the other is the least arbitrary and thus the most systematical. The former tends to use vocabulary as a tool and the latter tends to use grammar as a tool. The Chinese language belongs to the former type while the English language belongs to the latter. As a matter of fact, it is universally acknowledged that

Chinese is paratactic and English is hypotactic. Therefore, people need to take the context into account when decoding a Chinese text, and to understand an English text, they have to figure out the inner linguistic structure. Many factors contribute to the linguistic difficulties in legal translation, but hereby we will mainly elaborate on two of the most important factors—different modes of thinking and linguistic non-equivalence.

Different Modes of Thinking

The language people use also plays a part in the formation of their mode of thinking. This has been partly proved by Edward Sapir and Benjamin Whorf. According to the Sapir-Whorf Hypothesis (SWH), language and thought are interdependent with each other. The hypothesis is interpreted mainly in two different ways: a strong version and a weak one. While the strong version, called linguistic determinism, believes that the language patterns determine people's thinking and behavior, the weak one, called linguistic relativity, holds that the former influences the latter.

SWH is supported by some other linguists. Kaplan (2001), an American linguist, proves in his book *Cultural Thought Patterns in Intercultural Education* that people with different linguistic and cultural backgrounds tend to think in different patterns. Kaplan once adopted the following diagram to depict the different modes of thinking between several languages, including English and Chinese:

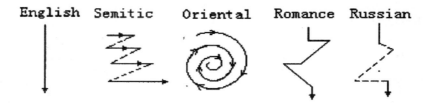

Kaplan points out that the thinking mode of English-speaking people is Aristotelian-linear whereas oriental thinking mode is circular or an approach by indirection as illustrated in the following diagram.

Chapter Four Legal Translation and Equivalence

 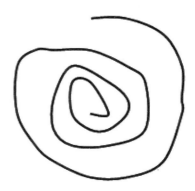

English Thinking Mode: Linear　　**Chinese Thinking Mode: Circular**

Chinese people are known by their intuitive, holistic, harmonious and dialectical mode of thinking. Chinese culture attaches great importance to the overall grasp of a phenomenon and intuitive perception of the implied. They tend to think from the whole to the part, and usually start from the general and then to the specific. This mode of thinking appears to be cyclical and synthetic. The native English speakers think right in the reverse order. They prefer to start from the part to the whole. This thinking mode is analytic and linear for native English speakers are good at logical inferences.

The difference is best illustrated by the different Chinese and English ways of expressing the address or the date. Some examples are given below:

地址：南京市鼓楼区北京东路1号

Address: No. 1, East Beijing Road, Gulou District, Nanjing City

2018年5月1日

1 May, 2018

The mode of thinking of a nation reflects its lingual and psychological tendencies formed in thousands of years, which will inevitably exert its influence on language translation, including legal translation. So how do the modes of thinking influence legal translation?

Firstly, the mode of thinking of Chinese people tends to be cyclical and

synthetic, while the thinking mode of native English speakers is analytic and linear, just as illustrated by the diagram above. Here is an example to prove that this difference in the mode of thinking exert a great influence on legal translation. The Chinese always use "provision" to denote "规定", or "regulation" to denote "条例". They think "XX条例" or "XX规定" is one single legal instrument, thus they tend to translate "本条例" or "本规定" into "this Regulation" or "this Provision." However, in fact, the native speakers of English are used to considering "regulation" or "provision" as "one article" of the whole law. Therefore, they generally use "these regulations" and "these provisions" to denote "本条例" and "本规定".

Secondly, the mode of thinking of Chinese people is more harmonious and dialectical than that of native English speakers. For instance, many Chinese idioms consist of both the positive and the negative sides, such as "悲喜交加" "是非曲直" "黑白分明" and so on. However, the English people, more often than not, will only mention one side of them, either positive or negative. For example, for its Chinese counterpart "权衡该方法的利弊", the English prefer to use the phrase "to evaluate the merits of the approach," with the negative side omitted. This difference is also reflected in the legalese. Take the following case for example: In Britain, there is an act called *Theft Act*. When rendering it into Chinese, a qualified legal translator will translate it into "反盗窃法" or "盗窃罪法" rather than a word-for-word version "盗窃法", for the latter is not in coincidence with the thinking mode of Chinese people.

Linguistic Non-equivalence

Probably the difficulty encountered initially by legal translators is the difference between languages, since different languages do not "mesh together." There is usually no full equivalence between code-units, and for the message to be equivalent in source text and target text, the code-units will be different since they belong to two different sign systems (language) which partition reality differently. For special-purpose communication, the text is formulated in a special language

Chapter Four Legal Translation and Equivalence

that is subject to special syntactic, semantic and pragmatic rules. According to White (1982: 423), one of the most problematic features of legal discourse is that it is invisible. He claims that the most serious obstacles to comprehensibility are not the vocabulary and sentence structure employed in law, but the unstated conventions by which language operates. Legal language has developed its characteristics to meet the demands of the legal system in which it is expressed. Linguistic difficulties often arise in translation from the differences found in the different legal cultures in the English Common Law and the Chinese Socialist Law. The root of the problem lies in their varying legal histories, cultures and systems.

To be more specific, a basic linguistic difficulty in legal translation is the absence of an exact correspondence across languages. For one thing, linguistic structures that are often found in English have no direct counterparts in Chinese. That is to say, the expression in the English legal texts carries concepts and ideas that simply do not exist in the Chinese vocabulary. For example, the Constitution of the United States establishes the *Principle of Federalism* in its legislative process and the system of *checks and balances.* The legislative power belongs to the *Congress*, which is made up of *the Senate* and *the House of Representatives.* All the above-mentioned terms appear so elementary in American legal culture, but are non-existent in Chinese legal system. For another, some legal terms in Chinese may superficially appear similar to those in English legal texts but in fact differ in meaning. If the translated version fails to represent lexical, syntactic features or stylistic flavor of the original one, it cannot be deemed equivalent with the source language. The use of these partial equivalents inevitably leads to meaning loss, which is often seen in current legal translation. For instance, professor Chen Zhongcheng (1998a: 78-80) discusses the translation of "trade secret" in his book *Window on Legal Translation.* He has questioned its commonly used translation "商业秘密". In fact, trade doesn't necessarily mean business or the commercial exchange, but may refer to any way of making a living—just like "trade" in "a jack of all trades." It includes, but is not limited to commerce. Therefore, "trade secret"

should be translated as "行业秘密" or "各行各业的秘密" or "业务秘密" in view of its connotation.

In terms of legal style, the languages of the Common Law and Civil law systems are fundamentally different in style. Legal traditions and legal cultures have had a lasting impact on the way law is written. Civil Law codes and statutes are concise while Common Law statutes are precise. (Tetley 2000:73) In the Civil Law system, statutes generally provide no definitions, and state principles in broad, general phrases. The interpretation of legal norm entails determining unforeseen and future problems. The thinking is abstract and system-oriented while the method is deductive. In contrast, in the Anglo-American context, statutes provide detailed definitions, and each specific rule sets out lengthy enumerations of specific applications or exceptions, preceded by a catch-all phrase and followed by qualifications. (Tetley 2000:73) The approach to legal problems is empirical. Consequently, legal writing in Common Law reflects the necessity to leave the judges as little room for interpretation as possible. This is most obvious in contracts between business partners. They result in wordy and lengthy texts, listing a seemingly endless array of terms with seemingly similar meanings. (Smith 1995) Typically, in an American contract, one finds phrases such as *any right, interest, title, property, ownership, entitlement and/ or any other claim…* The equivalent in Chinese would be one phrase "合法要求", meaning legal claims. The same is true for the language of court decisions. Common law judicial opinions are usually long and contain elaborate reasoning, whereas the legal opinions in China are usually short and more formal in nature and style.

In short, the differences between two legal systems and the consequent differences in the language used in law as described above have an impact on legal translation. The diverse range of linguistic differences is one of the most challenging aspects that confront the legal translators.

Chapter Four　Legal Translation and Equivalence

Legal Translational Equivalence: Possibility and Impossibility

As stated before, the translation of legal texts demands high degree of accuracy and coherence. A minor difference in meaning between the source text and the target text can lead to disastrous consequences, because every single word or expression in a legal text is of legal effect, which is not open to even the smallest misinterpretation. However, the questions of equivalence are especially problematic in the field of legal translation for various reasons. The lack of equivalence and the demand for high precision make a paradox. To explore this issue, we can look at it from the following perspectives.

Firstly, it is a fact that we translate legal texts between different legal traditions and legal systems, and we have been doing so for the past few centuries. Assisted by the process of translation, the laws and legal systems in many countries and continents have been developed on the basis of legal transplant from other legal families. Many foreign legal terminologies, concepts, practices have been introduced to China in this way. Take the new *Contract Law of PRC* promulgated in 1999 for example, there are many loan words like "无权处分""同时履行抗辩""不安抗辩""代位权""撤销权" etc., which come from German, Latin, English and other foreign languages. (Fang 2005: 17) Therefore, successful experience at that tells us translating legal texts, irrespective of what legal families are involved, is not only possible, but also high productive. Nevertheless, this does not mean that there are no problems or the job is easy.

Secondly, if we turn to the angle of translational equivalence, a number of factors need to be taken into account when legal concepts and practices in English legal texts are translated that have no exact equivalents in Chinese. Take the legal concepts for example, legal concepts from different countries are seldom, if ever, identical. This is because that The Nature of Language dictates that two words are

rarely the same between English and Chinese. Moreover, law is a human and social institution, established on the basis of the diverse moral and cultural values of individual societies. Each human society has its own political, cultural, and social conditions and circumstances and can never be duplicated. Of course, the other side of the same coin is that human societies do share many things in common. More things combine than divide us despite the differences. Some legal concepts may overlap in different societies but seldom identical. Therefore, it is useless to search for absolute equivalence when translating legal texts. As Toury (1986: 1123) observes, equivalence is a combination of, or compromise between, the two basic types of constraints that draw from the incompatible poles of the target system and the source text and system. In another word, translational equivalence is a relative notion.

Thirdly, the issue of interpretation and application of the translated legal texts, after the initial linguistic transfer, is also a related consideration. In the comprehending of translated texts originally written for different audiences in different languages, inevitably there are some confusions and misunderstandings. Naturally, it is necessary that legal translators establish a degree of equivalent relationship between the source language and target language to avoid such confusion. But what kind of equivalent relationship? As pointed out above, the translation of legal texts is a means of specialized communication under the mechanism of law. To make the legal communication effective, translators must bear the legal effect of the texts in mind throughout the translation process and try to guarantee its uniform interpretation and application in the target language. That is, equivalence in legal effect needs to be achieved and thus a function-oriented approach should be adopted.

Summing up, despite the seemingly insurmountable conceptual and linguistic gulf between different laws and languages, the translation of legal texts is possible, and legal communication can be realized.

Chapter Five

Theories and Principles for Legal Translation

The importance as well as the complexity and difficulty of legal translation, has long been recognized by legal translators. Extensive research has been carried out in this field, yet very few attempts have been made to apply the translation theories to the practice of legal translation. People used to think that legal translation could be done without any theoretical basis as long as translators were experienced in the practice. In fact, if there should be any improvement of translation quality in this field, it is important to select a systematic and appropriate translation theory to guide the practice.

In recent years, there has been a radical change in the perspective of translation theory. With the emergence of approaches centered on communicative and pragmatic factors, growing emphasis is now placed on translation as a communicative and intercultural action. The translator is no longer considered as a passive mediator but an intercultural operator, whose choices are not only based on linguistic criteria but also on other considerations, first and foremost the function of the translated text in the target culture. Therefore, this book attempts to discuss the applicability of Nida's functional equivalence theory to legal translation, and to specify the functional equivalence in legal translation.

法律翻译
LEGAL TRANSLATION

Functional Equivalence Theory

Eugene A. Nida, a distinguished American linguist and translation theorist, is regarded as the most influential one among all contemporary translation theorist. His translation theory has exerted a great influence on translation studies in western countries and even greater in China. "Dynamic equivalence" is a core concept in Nida's translation theory. It was first put forward in *Toward a Science of Translation* (1964) and elaborated in *The Theory and Practice of Translating* (1969). In the mid-1980s, "dynamic equivalence" was replaced by "functional equivalence" to avoid misunderstanding and to emphasize the concept of function. In the early 1990s, "functional equivalence" was further divided into two levels: the maximal level and the minimal level. It can be noted that "dynamic equivalence" has been developed and amended since it was first proposed.

Dynamic Equivalence

"Dynamic equivalence" derives from "the principle of equivalent effect" postulated by Rieu and Phillips. (Nida 1964: 159) In 1964, Nida distinguishes two types of equivalence: formal equivalence and dynamic equivalence. As defined by Nida (1964:59), formal equivalence focuses attention on the message itself, in both form and content. One is concerned that the message in the receptor language should match as closely as possible the different elements in the source language. Formal equivalence is text-oriented, which means that the message in the receptor culture is constantly compared with the message in the source culture to determine the standards of accuracy and correctness. A formal equivalent translation is a literal but meaningful translation, which usually requires footnotes in order to make the text fully comprehensible. (Ma 2003: 93) In contrast to formal equivalence, dynamic equivalence is reader-oriented. In such a translation, the translator is concerned about the dynamic relationship, that is, "the relationship between

Chapter Five   Theories and Principles for Legal Translation

receptors and message should be substantially the same as that which existed between the original receptors and the message" (Nida 1964:159). The message has to be tailored to the receptor's linguistic needs and cultural expectation and "aims at complete naturalness of expression" (Nida 1964:166). The above is the gist of Nida's two basic types of equivalence in translating. A translator can follow either of the two orientations to achieve the desired translation effect according to situational factors, and Nida does not consider one is superior to another in terms of the translation quality.

Not until 1969, Nida comes up with his "new concept of translating," shifting the focus from "the form of the message" to "the response of the receptor." In his book *The Theory and Practice of Translation* (1969), "dynamic equivalence" is defined as "in terms of the degree to which the receptors of the message in the receptor language respond to it in substantially the same manner as the receptors in the source language." In other words, the receptor's response to the translated message should be similar to that of the original receptor in the source language. Such response can never be identical, especially when the two cultural and historical setting are extremely different. Hence, Nida regards translating as reproducing in the receptor language the closest natural equivalent of the source-language message, first in terms of meaning, and secondly in terms of style. (Nida & Taber 1969: 12) This receptor-oriented approach suggests that the form should be restructured to preserve the same meaning.

What's more, it is necessary to notice that "formal equivalence" is not mentioned in his 1969 book. Instead, the concept of "formal correspondence" is put forward as opposed to "dynamic equivalence." Nida holds that "dynamic equivalence" should have priority over "formal correspondence," which is, in essence, related to a word-for-word translation. In Nida's translation theory, "formal equivalence" and "formal correspondence" are two different concepts. If we fail to discriminate the differences between them, it's easy to draw some wrong conclusions about "formal equivalence."

Functional Equivalence

Since the 1970s, "dynamic equivalence" has been further clarified and developed. In *From One Language to Another* (1986), the expression "dynamic equivalence" was changed to "functional equivalence." Essentially, there are not many differences between the two concepts. The substitution of "functional equivalence" is to avoid misunderstandings of the term "dynamic," which is often mistaken by some people for something in the sense of impact. (Nida 1993: 124) Meanwhile, it was designed to emphasize the communicative functions of translation. The terms "function" and "functional" seem to provide a much sounder basis for talking about translation as a form of communication.

Later, Nida (1993: 118) further develops "functional equivalence" by dividing it into two levels in *Language, Culture and Translation* and defines them as follows:

> [the minimal level] The readers of a translated text should be able to comprehend it to the point that they can conceive of how the original readers of the text must have understood and appreciated it.

> [the maximal level] The readers of a translated text should be able to understand and appreciate in it essentially the same manner as the original readers did.

Accordingly, the functional equivalence is stated primarily in terms of comparison of the way in which the original receptors comprehend and appreciate the original text and the way in which the intended receptors of the translated text comprehend and appreciate the translated text. Moreover, the adequacy of a translation depends on a great many different factors: the reliability of the text itself, the discourse type, the intended audience, the manner in which the translated text is to be used, and the purpose for which the transition has been made. In this case, the maximal level of functional equivalence is an ideal and is rarely achieved except for those texts of

Chapter Five Theories and Principles for Legal Translation

routine information, which have little or no aesthetic value; whereas the minimal level is realistic and a translation below this level is unacceptable (ibid).

"Functional equivalence" is very flexible, and there is a considerable range of adequacy from minimal to maximal effectiveness. A number of different translations can represent varying degrees of equivalence. This means that "equivalence" should not be understood in its mathematical meaning of identity, but only in terms of proximity, i.e., on the basis of degrees of closeness to functional identity. (Nida 1993: 117) Compared with some translation theories which attempt to set a single standard, functional equivalence allows a wide range of diversity in translation.

Principles for Producing Functional Equivalence

With the amendment of functional equivalence theory, Nida's attitude toward "formal correspondence" also alters to a certain degree. This change is more conspicuous in his later work *Language, Culture, and Translating* (1993), in which he lists several principles for translators to produce "functional equivalence":

(1) If a close, formal translation is likely to result in a misunderstanding of the designative meaning, certain changes must be introduced into the text of the translation or the literal translation may be retained and a footnote explaining the likely misunderstanding must be added.

(2) If a close, formal translation makes no sense, or in other words it is totally obscure in designative meaning, certain changes must be introduced into the text unless the source text is purposely obscure, in which case the obscurity may be retained, and a footnote explaining the nature of the obscurity may be very useful and in most instances fully justified.

(3) If a close, formal translation is so semantically and syntactically difficult that the average person for whom the translation is being made is very likely to give up trying to comprehend it, certain changes are warranted,

although it may be useful to indicate the nature of such changes in an introduction or in footnotes.

(4) If a close, formal translation is likely to result in serious misunderstanding of the associative meanings of the source text or in a significant loss in a proper appreciation for the stylistic values of the source text, it is important to make such adjustments as are necessary to reflect the associative values of the source text.

(5) The manner in which a translation is to be used has a significant influence upon the extent to which adjustments are to be made.

(6) The fact that a source text must be translated in such a way as to occur with accompanying codes usually requires a number of adjustments on all levels: phonology, lexicon, syntax, and discourse. (1993: 125-129)

Looking at these principles from another perspective, we may say that a formal translation may be adequate except for the six special cases. Whether a formal translation is acceptable or not depends on the adequacy of translation in terms of functional equivalence. That is to say, if a more or less literal correspondence is functionally equivalent in both designative and associative meaning, then obviously no adjustments in form are necessary. (ibid)

Dual Equivalence and Ideal Equivalence: Application of Functional Equivalence Theory to Legal Translation

Nida's functional equivalence theory developed from his abundant experience of Bible translation. The main function of Bible is to preach the Christian doctrine to its believers, telling them what is advocated and what is prohibited. When performing this work, Nida is aware that Bible is directly bound with

Chapter Five   Theories and Principles for Legal Translation

religious effect. The translated version of Bible should be as "holy" as the original one; otherwise the religious effect would be lost. Consequently, Nida uses the "receptors' response" as a parameter to guide his Bible translation. That is to make the Christian believers react correspondingly when they read the Word of God. This theory has been widely adopted by Bible translators and has been proved successful. Since biblical texts belong to special-purpose texts, can functional equivalence theory be applied to the translation of other special-purpose texts, such as legal texts? In other words, is it legitimate to propose the application of functional equivalence theory to legal translation?

It is clear that functional approach takes into account all of the basic elements involved in the process of translating, namely, the source, the message and the receptor, thus it tends to be more descriptive and neutral and is more likely to provide a satisfactory guideline. The production of equivalent messages is a process, not only of matching the parts of utterances, but also of reproducing the total dynamic character of communication. The great contribution Nida has made is to shift the focus from the comparison of a pair of texts (the source text and the target text), to a comparison of the two communication process. This new method of comparison doesn't mean that the importance of the text can be ignored, since the message in a communication is conveyed by means of the text. Instead, the shift of focus implies the consideration of various linguistic and cultural factors that can affect the receptors' perception of the message in the text. Seen from these perspectives, Nida's theory of functional equivalence is applicable and significant to the translation of legal texts.

Legal translation is a communication process performed within the mechanism of law, in which the "receptors' response" is of vital importance. It is possible to visualize the "receptors' response" of the original legal text and the translated legal text, because most of the legal texts will lead to a series of actions of the receptors in reality. If the target language receptors do not perform exactly as the source language receptors, there shall be some mistakes in the translated legal texts. It

shows that the translator fails to transfer the correct message of the source legal texts and this kind of translation is totally without practical use.

As for the "conflict" between the traditional notions of content and form, Nida (1964: 164) underlines that "correspondence in meaning must have priority over correspondence in style" if equivalent effect is to be achieved. This assertion is in line with the goal of legal translation. Undoubtedly, the most important criterion of legal translation is to maintain the communicative function of the original texts in the target language. If the translated version doesn't achieve the intended legal effect, the translation would not be regarded as acceptable, even if the form, aesthetics and readability are conveyed appropriately. As a result, achieving equivalence in legal effect between the two texts is always the translator's top priority. It doesn't constitute a contradiction between taking functional equivalence as the main task and considering the stylistic correspondence as the secondary, but a necessary action. As a translation theory in linguistic tradition, functional equivalence meets the need to achieve a balance between faithfulness and the effect of translated works.

However, legal translation is much more complicated as it involves not only two distinct languages, but also two different legal systems. It should be noted that the translation of legal texts is a double operation, in which the language transfer and legal transfer are conducted at the same time. This is the essence of principle of dual functional equivalence put forward by Mr Zhu Dingchu (2002), including two essential requirements: equivalence in linguistic effects and equivalence in legal effects. It is improper to apply this general translation theory to it without any modification. Due to the lack of equivalence, special compensation strategies are required to achieve both linguistic equivalence and legal equivalence.

Essentials of Dual Equivalence and Ideal Equivalence

Based on Nida's functional equivalence theory, the goal of translating legal texts can be further elaborated as the three presumptions: (a) the content, the

Chapter Five Theories and Principles for Legal Translation

meaning or the statement in target language texts (TLT) should be equivalent to that in source language texts (SLT), (b) the legal effect in the TLT should be equivalent to that in SLT, (c) the intended readers should understand and appreciate the TLT as the original readers do.

Like Nida's functional equivalence, the adequacy of TLT changes in degree on the basis of both cognitive and experiential factors. Referring to the two levels of functional equivalence divided by Nida, Li Ziheng (2009:27) presents two definitions of equivalence in translating legal texts:

[Dual Equivalence] At least, TLT can make the intended receptor comprehend it to the point that they can conceive how the original reader of SLT must have understood and appreciated the content and the legal effect.

[Ideal Equivalence] If possible, TLT can make the intended receptor understand and appreciate the content and the legal effect in essentially the same manner as the original reader did.

Similarly, ideal equivalence can be rarely achieved in practice while dual equivalence is realistic and a translation less than this degree is unacceptable.

To specify the dual equivalence in the translation process, it is necessary to construct and analyze a model for legal translation. Here, some symbols are used to make it clear. Define the content or the statement of SLT as $M1$ (M stands for message), the legal effect as $M2$ and the combination of the two as $M3$. In the same way, define the content or the legal statement, legal effect and the combination in TLT as $M1'$, $M2'$, and $M3'$. First, the translator reads the SLT and gets a thorough understanding of the content $M1$ and legal effect $M2$. Second, the translator attempts to transfer them into the proper $M1'$ and $M2'$ in the target language and legal system. Last, the translator synthesizes them into $M3'$ and restructures it to produce TLT. If the intended receptor can decode $M1'$ and $M2'$ from it, the translation is successful and dual equivalence has been achieved.

Unfortunately, this is not always the case. If the translator fails to transfer the correct legal effect $M2$ into $M2'$, what is decoded by the intended receptor often

leads to misunderstandings and wrong reactions, even though the content M1' can be understood by the intended reader. This kind of translation is unacceptable and has no practical use. If the translator fails to transfer the proper content M1, such as producing a rigid word-for-word literal translation, the TLT will be hard to understand and the intended receptor may get nothing from it. What's even worse, if the translation fails to convey both the content M1 and legal effect M2, this kind of TLT is completely useless.

Principles for Application to Legal Translation

A preliminary model for translating legal texts has been constructed and the circumstances in which the dual equivalence can be achieved have been analyzed above. Still, it is insufficient for legal translators to achieve the goal of the translating legal texts. Because it is just an abstract model and analysis of translation process, some basic principles for its application must be added. Again, just as the principles presented by Nida to produce "functional equivalence," some principles are required to guide the production of dually equivalent legal texts:

(1) Legal language is a technical language with its own distinctive features. The translator should try to make sure that TLT has the same linguistic characteristics as the SLT, such as formality, preciseness, conciseness and all that. These principles are of great significance in standardizing the translation of legal texts and can be used as a reference for legal translators.

(2) Legal texts have specific social function and practical value. The translator should correctly transfer the content and legal effect in legal communication. He is free to choose literal translation or liberal translation to achieve equivalence, but the fidelity to the legal effect should be given priority.

If a close, literal translation is likely to result in a misunderstanding of the content and legal effect, the equivalence in legal effect is the first priority. Accordingly, certain changes must be introduced into the TLT or the literal

Chapter Five   Theories and Principles for Legal Translation

translation may be retained and a footnote explaining the likely misunderstanding must be added.

If a close, literal translation is so semantically and syntactically difficult that the average receptor is very likely to give up trying to comprehend it, certain changes are warranted, although it may be useful to indicate the nature of such changes in an introduction or in footnotes.

(3) The translation of legal texts is not only a cross-language communication act, but also a cross-cultural and cross-legal-system one. The translator should seek common grounds while reserving differences when making a comparative study of the different languages, cultures and legal systems. If it is impossible to find exact equivalents, the translator should make up for it by using footnotes or paraphrase to make the statement understandable for target language receptor.

Basic Principles for Legal Translation

Many scholars, both at home and abroad, have developed many translation principles from the long-term translation practice. They are trying to define criteria to be used by translators when selecting a translation strategy. In China, one of the most famous translation principles is the criteria—"faithfulness, expressiveness, and elegance" put forward by Yan Fu in the preface to his translation of *Evolution and Ethics*. According to him, a good translation is one that is true to the original in spirit, accessible to the target reader in meaning, and attractive to the target reader in style. In 1952, Fu Lei held that translation is like painting: what is essential is not formal resemblance but rather spiritual resemblance. In 1964, Qian Zhongshu believed that the highest standard of translation is transformation, that is, bodies are sloughed off, but the spirit, appearance and manner are the same as before. Foreign scholars have also made valuable contributions to the development of the principles. Tytler laid down three main principles in his book *Essay on the*

LEGAL TRANSLATION

Principles of Translation (1978), that is, the translation should give a complete transcript of the idea of the original work; the style and manner of writing should be of the same character with that of the original; and the translation should have all the ease of the original composition. Eugene A. Nida's most notable contribution to translation theory is Dynamic Equivalence, also known as Functional Equivalence, which has just been introduced in this chapter.

As a special branch of translation, legal translation must follow some unique translation principles as well as the above mentioned principles. This part mainly elaborates on four principles for legal translation: precision and accuracy, consistency and identity, professionalism and standardization, clarity and standardization.

Principle of Accuracy and Precision

Law is a system of rules that are created and enforced through social or governmental institutions to regulate behavior, which ensures that individuals or a community adhere to the will of the state. To enable people to better understand the contents and comply with these provisions, the statements in the laws must be clear and unambiguous. The more precise and unambiguous the terms, the greater the degree of legal certainty. Otherwise, lawless people may exploit a loophole in the law to avoid legal liabilities.

Of the principles for general translation, "faithfulness" means that the translation must be completely loyal to the original text. Similarly, legal translation is also bound by the principle of fidelity. Legal translators must be absolutely faithful to the original text and cautious enough to avoid any emotional judgment. Any distortion, lack of fidelity, or ambiguity of the law is likely to cause legal accidents, and hence, incur serious legal consequences. The following clause from a "will" is a good example.

The remainder of the testator's property should be divided equally between

Chapter Five   Theories and Principles for Legal Translation

our 22 nephews and nieces on my wife's side and my niece.

How can the property be divided according to the clause? Shall it be divided into two halves, one for the testator's only niece and the other for the 22 nephews and nieces on the wife's side, or shall it be divided into 23 equal parts, one for each person? The use of preposition "between" instead of "among" shows the testator's intent to divide the property into two halves. But the clients would not have gone to the law if the original will had been written as follows:

The remainder of the testator's property should be divided equally between all of our nephews and nieces on my wife's side as one party and my niece as the other.

Therefore, accuracy is the primary principle of legal translation as well as the fundamental characteristic of legal language.

Principle of Consistency and Identity

For literary translation, translators may choose synonyms to express the same idea, for the sake of diversity of vocabulary instead of repeating the same term. However, even a slight difference between two synonyms may cause ambiguity in legal language. Therefore, it is necessary to maintain the identity of a legal term when referring to the same legal concept in one legal text.

Different from literary translation, once the word is chosen in the legislative text, it must be used throughout the entire translation process. Consistency is also one basic principle to observe in legal translation as it can further guarantee the accuracy of the translation work. Weihofen (1961: 58) said in his *Legal Writing Style*, "Exactness often demands repeating the same term to express the same idea. Where that is true, never be afraid of using the same word over and over again. Many more sentences are spoiled by trying to avoid repetition than by repetition." For example, *mediation* and *conciliation* are synonyms and both of them can be translated into Chinese as "调解". But if the word *mediation* is used at the very beginning, the translator should use that term consistently, rather than using *conciliation* in the same meaning.

法律翻译
LEGAL TRANSLATION

Apart from keeping terms consistent within the same document, the translator should refer to the higher laws and relevant government documents to ensure the consistency between the legal text and its higher laws. Lack of consistency may result in adverse effect on the information delivery as readers may unnecessarily surmise that differences exist between such terms or even question the professionalism of the provisions.

To put it more clearly, the identity principle means using the same word or term to express the same concept or idea, and the consistency principle demands repeating the same word or term, especially the key word or term, throughout the whole document, and at the same time, using the same definition of the word or term as is used in the governing laws concerned. Use of synonyms or near-synonyms would otherwise have resulted in litigation confusion, though it might make the language less drab.

The following two examples will illustrate this principle in detail.

Example 1

Original: ……被告（宝洁公司）从未以任何方式向原告（雇员）施加精神压力。被告可以拿走原告的文档和他使用的电脑，这是公司的规章制度所规定的，其目的是防止公司的商业秘密被泄露。

Translation: ... the defendant (P&G) never exerted any spiritual pressure in any form on the **claimant**. The defendant was free to take away all the **plaintiff's** files and the computer he had been using, strictly in accordance with the company's stipulations, and that such actions were aimed at preventing the company's trade secrets from being disclosed.

In the translated version above, two different terms are used for "原告": "claimant" and "plaintiff," which is inappropriate in legal translation, for in this way, the readers may mistake the two terms for two different entities. The translation can be improved as follows:

Improved Translation: ... the defendant (P&G) never exerted any spiritual pressure in any form on the plaintiff. In accordance with the company's stipulations,

Chapter Five   Theories and Principles for Legal Translation

the defendant was entitled to/had the right to take away the plaintiff's files and the computer the plaintiff had used in order to prevent the company's trade secrets from being disclosed.

Example 2

Original: 保税区的减免税货物、保税货物的监管手续费，应当按照《中华人民共和国海关对进口减税、免税和保税货物征收海关监管手续费的办法》办理。

Translation: The Customs supervising fees on the import goods granted with duty reduction and exemption and that on the **goods in bond** shall be collected in accordance with the *Customs Regulations of the People's Republic of China Governing the Collection of Customs Supervising Fees on Import Goods Granted with Duty Reduction or Exemption and the **Bonded Goods.***

Comparing the English translation with the original, we find that both "goods in bond" and "Bonded Goods" refer to the same concept "保税货物". Although both versions are acceptable here, translators are encouraged to repeat the same term to express the same concept in order to keep consistent and identical and to avoid leaving loopholes in legal articles and clauses.

Principle of Professionalism and Standardization

Legislative documents regulate the interests and rights of concerning parties under the jurisdiction, which strictly requires standardized and precise expression. People need to learn the specific connotation and boundary of the interests and rights prescribed in the provisions and determine the code of conducts according to these documents. Therefore, rigorous diction, normal terms and specified sentence patterns are the essential characteristics of legislative texts and the translator must observe the principle of standardization during the translation process.

In literary works, the translator usually uses particular languages such as dialects and slangs to show different language styles. However, it is forbidden to do

法律翻译
LEGAL TRANSLATION

so in legal translation as legal language is of the highest degree of formality and it is applicable to all regions under its jurisdiction. The style of legal language is often described as sacred and solemn. Therefore, the translator must choose standardized words or official language and avoid the use of oral language or dialects. For example, "章" "部" "条" "款" "段" "节" should be translated respectively as *chapter, part, section, subsection, paragraph* and *subparagraph*.

On many occasions, mistakes occur because translators take the meaning of the original texts too literally. For example, in a Chinese case report, the Chinese legal term "强奸未遂" was rendered by someone as *try to rape for a short time and then fail* instead of *an attempted rape*. Though the literal translation carries the meaning, it is not acceptable to legal professionals. Likewise, *a cautioned statement* should be translated into "警戒供词" rather than "谨慎的声明" or "告诫书".

Here are some commonly used legal terms and their standard translation.

action	诉讼	demise	遗赠，转让
avoidance	宣告无效	executed	签名生效
check	牵制，制约，支票	hand	签名
consideration	对价，约因	securities listing	证券上市
construction	解释	the delisting of the company	上市公司被摘牌
discovery	调查证据	master	雇主
effects	财物、财产	motion	动议，提案
execution	合同等的签订	offer	要约
fee	可继承不动产	party	当事人
instrument	票据	retainer fee	律师费
limitation	时效	damages	赔偿金

Chapter Five   Theories and Principles for Legal Translation

（续表）

minor	未成年人	interest	权益
omission	不作为	issue	子女
principal	主犯；当事人；被代理人，本人	prayer	诉讼请求
title	所有权、产权书	prejudice	损害合法权利
abstract	无因性	counterpart	副本
alien	转让、让渡	serve	送达
avoid	使无效、废止	save	除……之外
battery	殴击	specialty	盖印合同/契约
dishonour	拒付	said	上述的

The principle of professionalism and standardization for legal translation does not apply to lexical items only. It also concerns the translation of syntactical structures, and some patterns and expressions used in legal documents, such as *without prejudice to..., subject to..., for the purpose of, where-clause* and so on. Besides, professionalism also demands that translators understand the real implication of each legal concept. For instance, *tax, tariff, duty, and levy* can all be translated into "税" or "税收", but they are different as far as legal concept is concerned.

Principle of Clarity and Concision

As is known to all, legal English has its unique stylistic features, which is full of obscure and rigid expressions. However, people argue that a law system concerned to safeguard ordinary people's rights should be written in a language that those people can understand, and this is precisely the aim of the pressure groups who are behind the Plain English Campaign. The simplified legal English

has its lexical and syntactical features such as more working words (which communicate your message) used instead of glue words (which stick the working words together to form a sentence); single words used instead of compound constructions; avoidance of the redundant legal phrases; use of base verbs instead of nominalization; avoidance of archaisms; use of familiar, common words instead of big words; avoidance of sexist languages, etc . Therefore, the principle of clarity and concision should be complied in legal translation, giving a lot of information in a few words.

The following is an example from an appellate brief, in which the writer is attempting to persuade the court that the district court made a mistake of interpretation.

> The district court, on the other hand, erroneously addressed but one word of the Banker's Blanket Bond—the term "realized"—and then the district court misapplied it by erroneously considering whether (the appellant) "realized" a benefit and the Bank suffered a loss, which is not a question under the Bankers Blanket Bond; and once the district court found that the Bank suffered a loss, it held the Insurer liable without considering the language of the Banker's Blanket Bond as relevant to the issue of whether that loss was covered under the Banker's Blanket Bond.

The above overburdened sentence is indeed bewildering. In fact, the sentence contains the following four crucial points:

(1) The court read only a part of the Banker's Blanket Bond.

(2) The court read that part incorrectly.

(3) As a consequence, the court failed to focus on the proper issue in the case.

(4) The dispositive issue in the case is whether the loss was covered under the Bond.

Chapter Five Theories and Principles for Legal Translation

Since each point is central to the writer's argument, a separate expression is preferred. The improved version is as follows:

The district court addressed only the term "realized" as used in the Bankers Blanket Bond. Then the court considered whether the appellee "realized" a benefit and the Bank suffered a loss. At that point, the court incorrectly held the Insurer liable. The issue is whether that loss was covered under the Bond.

However, it is not always easy to be perfect in both clarity and concision. In this case, it is preferable to be wordier so as to achieve clarity, i.e., without distorting nuances of meaning implied in the original. Now compare the Chinese and English versions of the following article:

In subsection (1) "complainant" means a woman upon whom, in a charge for a rape offence or indecent assault to which the trial in question relates, it is alleged that rape or indecent assault was committed, attempted or proposed.

在第(1)款中，"上诉人"(complainant)指在有关审讯关乎的强奸罪行或猥亵侵犯的控罪中，指称遭人强奸和猥亵侵犯，或指称遭人企图强奸或猥亵侵犯，或指称有人打算将其强奸或对其猥亵侵犯的女子。

In the English original, the clause—it is alleged that rape or indecent assault was committed, attempted or proposed—is rendered into three sentences in Chinese: 指称遭人强奸和猥亵侵犯，或指称遭人企图强奸或猥亵侵犯，或指称有人打算将其强奸或对其猥亵侵犯. It seems wordy, but without repeating the same expression, the meaning contained in the original would not have been communicated clearly. Here the priority is given to precision.

Chapter Six

Legal Terminological Issues in Translation

Legal terminology is the most conspicuous and distinctive linguistic feature of legal language, and it is one of the major sources of difficulty in legal translation. The legal vocabulary, including both legal concepts and legal usage, is extensive in a legal language. It results from and reflects a particular legal system that utilizes the language. In this chapter, major terminological issues and problems in legal translation are examined.

Translating Legal Concepts

A concept is an idea or abstract principle of an object. It involves an abstract image created by the human mind on the basis of the features peculiar to a thing or matter. Legal concepts are abstraction of the legal rules and thoughts within a legal system. Concepts are of great importance in law. Law does not exist in the physical world, but is entirely created by humans. It is always related to the culture of a particular society, and therefore constitutes a social phenomenon. Because of this correlation, legal rules differ in different legal orders, so do legal concepts.

As a consequence, a frequently encountered challenge in legal translation

Chapter Six   Legal Terminological Issues in Translation

is the translation of legal concepts, which are often legal system-bound. In many other specialized fields, such as mathematics, chemistry, and physics, most technical terms have a relatively close equivalent in other languages. The reason is that the fields themselves are international, and often the critical concepts are also international. Law, on the other hand, differs in many aspects from one jurisdiction to the other. Even within a single language, such as English, there are some significant differences between British English and American usage, and sometimes even in the usage of various American states. Where the concepts of two legal systems differ, the semantic domains of legal terminology do not correspond with one another. Due to the differences between English and Chinese legal systems, the legal translator has to deal with the problem of terminological incongruency.

The problem of terminological incongruency is not new. Efforts have been made to cope with this difficulty. For instance, as Lane reports (see also Cao 2008: 54), the International Institute of Legal and Administrative Terminology attempted to tackle the problem arising from the translation of legal concepts that are unknown in the target language or that do not exist in exactly the same form as in that language. The institution made a terminological comparison between one language and the other based on concepts and terms, and then compiled and published volumes of *European Glossary of Legal and Administrative Terminology* with detailed description and comparison of various legal and administrative terminology in different European languages.

Sarcevic (1997: 238) proposes three categories of equivalence for translators in the field of law: near equivalence, partial equivalence, and non-equivalence. Cao (2008: 55) argues that a legal concept is three dimensional based on Peirce's semiotics, that is linguistic, referential and conceptual dimensions. He analyzes two major scenarios in translation: firstly, when there are no existing equivalent concepts in the target language, that is, they are linguistically and conceptually absent, new words must be created or new meanings introduced; and secondly, when there are existing words in the target language that are linguistic equivalent to

the source language, these words may only carry partially equivalent meanings in law or may not functionally equivalent in law at all, which can be seen conceptually and referentially absent.

Accordingly, different translation strategies can be adopted in line with the degree of equivalence. When legal concepts are equivalent, use the exact equivalents in the target language. When legal concepts are nearly or partially equivalent, many different methods may be utilized, given the vast differences and diverse situations, such as lexical expansion, descriptive paraphrases etc. When legal concepts are totally different, borrowing and neologism are much more common methods.

Focusing on the Meaning of Legal Terminology

Ordinary Meaning vs. Legal Meaning

As we can see, a legal term can just be a word or phrase that only appears in legal language like *tort, limitation of action, the burden of proof, criminal responsibility*, which can't be replaced by other words or be arbitrarily extended in meaning. It can also be a word or phrase that forms part of ordinary language but that has a special meaning in legal language. For instance, the most common meaning of *instrument* is a device for making music, or a tool for doing a scientific task, but lawyers use it to refer to a document (usually one that is performative).

This can sometimes be very confusing for laypeople, who might think that they understand a word or phrase when they do not. For example, legal terms that frequently appear in contract law include *offer, consideration, performance, remedy* and *assignment*. These words in English have an ordinary meaning used in non-legal context, but they are also legal technical terms that have special legal significance. In English contract law, *offer* refers to an indication of willingness to

Chapter Six Legal Terminological Issues in Translation

do or refrain from doing something that when accepted constitutes an agreement. *Consideration* refers to the price paid, rather than the careful thought. *Performance* of contract refers to the carrying out of obligations under a contract. *Remedy* is not just a way of dealing with a problem, but a legal means for the enforcement, protection, or recovery of rights or for obtaining redress for their infringement. The word *assignment* in contract law means the transfer of property or right, not just a task or piece of work that you are given to do.

Therefore, one of the tasks for the legal translator is to identify the legal meaning and distinguish it from its ordinary meaning before translating it appropriately into the target language.

Legal Polysemy

Legal terminology is characterized by polysemy, which means a single term can express several concepts depending on the context. Although polysemy causes difficulties, it allows the vocabulary of the language to transmit the infinitely varied ideas and feelings that arise in social life. (Vlasenko 1997: 48, quoted by Matilla 2006:109) The phenomenon of polysemy is basically explained by the fact that legal orders are continually changing over time.

To take *civil law* as an example, the term, derived from the Latin words *"jus civile,"* has at least four meanings nowadays. First, it refers to Roman law sometimes. Second, it denotes continental laws (strongly influenced by Roman law), as distinct from the English system of common law. Thirdly, it refers to private law, the branch of law in a civil law legal system that governs relations among private individuals, as opposed to public law, military law, and ecclesiastical law. Lastly, it may refer to municipal law, the domestic law of a state, as opposed to international law.

Where polysemy occurs, the legal translator should be able to assign to the term the meaning appropriate to the context. They should be aware of the fact that the term may also have other meanings besides the one that first comes to their

法律翻译
LEGAL TRANSLATION

mind. Given that the phenomenon of polysemy is very common, the legal translator should always be alert to it.

Legal Synonyms

Synonymy as a phenomenon is opposite to polysemy: two or several terms express the same concept. Synonymy is also a striking linguistic feature of legal terms. A legal term may have several synonyms and some of them may resemble each another, but differ in legal meaning. For instance, there are so many words related to law— *law, statute, legislation, act, enactment, regulation, rule, decree* etc.

Synonymy contributes to the accuracy of legal language. Synonyms and quasi-synonyms of the legal term, guarantee that the law or document covers all the intended cases or eventualities. For example, a will may read as follows: I give, devise and bequeath the rest, residue and remainder of my estate to Samantha. (Tiersma 1999: 64-65) The words *rest, residue* and *remainder* do not differ from the legal standpoint; nor do the words *give, devise* and *bequeath*. The sentence could simply have been put like this: *I give the rest of my estate to Samantha.*

In translation practice, partial synonyms are especially misleading. In general, misunderstandings and misinterpretations are possible where the semantic fields of two terms stand side by side. Moreover, it may be difficult to find sufficient synonyms in the target language. This may pose a challenge to the legal translator who needs to be resourceful and even creative so that he/she can make appropriate choices to differentiate the synonyms.

Problems in the Translation of Legal Terminology in China

With the deepening of reform and opening up, China is increasingly participating in international political, economic and cultural communications. As a means of

Chapter Six Legal Terminological Issues in Translation

legal communication, legal translation has played an increasingly important role in our globalized world. In recent years, we have made remarkable achievements in translating laws, but there are still some problems in the translation of legal technical terms.

Take the Words too Literally, Mistaking General Terms for Technical Terms

The translation of legal terminology involves selecting appropriate technical terms in the target language. The selected legal terms need to reflect the essential features of the alleged legal concepts. The legal translator can't take the words too literally and discard their legal effect. For example, in the *English-Chinese Vocabulary Handbook on Chinese Laws and Regulations* published in 1998, the term "物证" is translated into *material evidence*. In this English version, the "material" literally corresponds to "物", while "evidence" corresponds to "证". The translation seems correct, but in fact the meaning of the term goes far beyond the original meaning. According to *Black's Law Dictionary*, the term *material evidence* actually refers to "evidence having some logical connection with the consequential facts or the issues," which can be verbal evidence or physical evidence. The "物证" in Chinese has an equivalent legal term in English—*real evidence*. Therefore, the word "material" in "material evidence" does not mean a substance, but means "(the evidence) that is directly relevant and important in a legal argument." It is in this sense that the translation of "material evidence" should be "实质上的证据" or "实质性证据" (Dong 2011: 56).

Another example is that some translators use *the third party* to translate the Chinese legal term "第三者" (the other man or the other woman involved in a marriage). In fact, *the third party* refers to "第三人" "第三方" (The third party in a civil action is neither an accuser nor a defendant, but the outcome of the case will affect his/her interest. Thus, he/she may file a request to join the litigation or the court may notify him/her to join the litigation) . However, "第三者" in Chinese

refers to the person who is involved in the intervention, interference and destruction of the legal marriage of others, either male or female, married or unmarried. (Chen 2000:67)

Not Know the Legal Cultures and Linguistic Features, Confusing One Legal Term with Another

If they are not familiar with the two legal systems and legal cultures, legal translators tend to confuse one legal term with another. For example, *reckless driving* is usually translated into "危险驾驶罪" (dangerous driving). In English, reckless driving is the criminal offense of operating a motor vehicle in a manner that shows conscious indifference to the safety of others. It is the operation of an automobile under such circumstances and in such a manner as to show a willful or reckless disregard of consequences. In such cases the driver displays a wanton disregard for the rules of the road; often misjudges common driving procedures and causes accidents and other damages. It is usually a more serious offense than careless driving, improper driving, or driving without due care and attention and is often punishable by fines, imprisonment, and/ or driver's license suspension or revocation. (Garner 2009:1385) In Chinese, "危险驾驶罪" refers to the drunk driving on the road, or the behavior of driving to chase if the circumstances are serious. By comparison, we can find that there are great differences between the definitions and connotations of the two legal terms. So, can we translate it into another Chinese legal term "交通肇事罪" (traffic accident crime) ? It means the behavior of violating regulations governing traffic and transportation and thereby causing a serious accident, which results in serious injuries or deaths or heavy losses of public or private property. Obviously, they are not the same in the meaning. Therefore, it is better to translate it into a new term "鲁莽驾驶罪". (Zhang 2016: 101-102)

The differences between two legal languages also play an important part in legal translation. For instance, Article 5 of the *Law of the People's Republic of*

Chapter Six   Legal Terminological Issues in Translation

China on Chinese-Foreign Equity Joint Ventures stipulates that "如果有意以落后技术和设备进行欺骗，造成损失，应赔偿损失。" There is one English version like this: "If it causes <u>losses</u> by deception through the intentional use of backward technology and equipment, the foreign joint venture shall pay compensation for the <u>losses</u>." In this version, loss is spelt in its plural form. There is no distinction of singular and plural forms in Chinese, whereas it's quite obvious in English. "损失" can be singular or plural in Chinese. Therefore, it is necessary to use *loss or losses* or *loss(es)* in the English version. (Li & Zhang 2006: 112)

Not Attach Importance to the Standardization of Translation, Misunderstanding the Connotation of Legal Terms

Some legal translators translate the same legal concept in the source language into different legal terms in the target language. For example, in the English version of *Copyright Law of the People's Republic of China*, "侵犯" is translated into *prejudice* (e.g., in Article 12) and *infringe* (e.g., in Article 48). However, according to the definitions and examples given by several English dictionaries, the emphasis of *infringe* is on the violation of rights, whereas *prejudice* is more on the violation of people, things and the interests. An example of the usage of the word *infringe* is found on page 549 in *Modern Advanced English-Chinese Dictionary*, published by Oxford University Press in 1978. It is quoted as "infringe a rule (an oath, copyright, a patent)." It is clear that the term *infringe* is mainly associated with the interference with the intellectual property rights. The example of the usage of the word *prejudice* on page 826 in the dictionary refers to an infringement of "any existing right or claim," which is more general in meaning.

Take the translation of "共同责任" and "连带责任" for example, the legal translator must distinguish the connotation of the two legal terms. In accordance with relevant provisions of the *Civil Law of China*, "共同责任" refers to the liability that is owed to a third party by two or more other parties together. It can be divided into two categories: "连带责任" and "按份责任". If people should bear

"连带责任", a claimant may pursue an obligation against any one party as if they were jointly liable and it becomes the responsibility of the defendants to sort out their respective proportions of liability and payment. This means that if the claimant pursues one defendant and receives payment, that defendant must then pursue the other obligors for a contribution to their share of the liability. (Dong 2015: 109) If people have "按份责任", the parties are liable for only their respective obligations. Therefore, "共同责任" should be translated as *joint liability*, while "连带责任" as *joint and several liability* and "按份责任" as *pro-portionate liability*.

Chapter Seven

Translation Competence and Techniques for Legal Translation

In the above chapters, a theoretical framework has been provided for legal translation. Like the law itself, a theory of legal translation needs to be practice-oriented so that it can be useful for translators. To put it into practice, the legal translator has a crucial role to play. No translation can depart from the translator's decoding of the source text, or the expression of the target text. The competence of the legal translator will directly determine the quality of the translation. Meanwhile, in view of the numerous restrictions in legal translation, special methods and techniques are required to guarantee the reliability. This chapter will illustrate the translation competence of the legal translator and the translation strategies employed to achieve dual equivalence in legal translation.

Translation Competence of the Legal Translator

Translation competence refers to the knowledge that is essential to the translation act. Many requirements have been offered of what the legal translator should be like and what skills the legal translator should possess. It is often said

that legal translation requires special knowledge, skills and experience on the part of the translator. Smith (1995: 181) believes that there are three prerequisites for successful translation of legal texts: the legal translator (1) must acquire a basic knowledge of the legal systems, both in SL and TL; (2) must possess familiarity with relevant terminology; and (3) must be competent in the TL-specific legal writing style. According to Sarcevic (1997:87), the legal translator traditionally acted as a mediator between text producers and receivers in a sterile triadic relationship. It was not until the twentieth century that the legal translator succeeded in converting his/her passive role in the communication process into an active one, finally emerging as text producer with new authority and responsibility. The legal translator is expected to preserve the unity of the single instrument by producing a text that expresses the uniform intent, i.e., the original intent of the lawmakers (legislation), States parties (treaties), or contracting parties (contracts). (Sarcevic 1997:87)

Consequently, legal translation is interdisciplinary in nature and the translator need a certain amount of expertise in many aspects. The competence of the legal translator can be identified and specified, and more importantly, can be learned and developed.

Linguistic Competence

Translation is a special type of communicative language use because it requires language competence in both the source language and the target language. This indicates that linguistic competence is a prerequisite for a translator. In this case, the translator is supposed to have a high level of proficiency in the receptive and productive skills in both English and Chinese. Different languages have distinctive features in lexis and syntax. For example, legal English has a propensity to use certain lexical and syntactical features such as archaic words and word strings, and long and complex structures. It would be a mistake to underestimate the linguistic difficulties this situation causes the legal translator. Thus, the legal

Chapter Seven Translation Competence and Techniques for Legal Translation

translator needs to be highly sensitive to the peculiar linguistic features of the legal texts. On one hand, they must be good readers, who can fully understand and appropriately decode the message of the English legal texts; on the other hand, they must be excellent writers, who can use proper expressions in Chinese to deliver the source meaning to the target receptors. And vice versa. In short, the linguistic competence is the ability to utilize, relate and mediate the two languages in the total communicative act of translation to achieve communicative goals.

Knowledge Structures

Though it is a linguistic activity, translation also requires adequate knowledge of the subject matter, i.e., translational knowledge structures, which are defined as the knowledge that is fundamental to achieve interlingual and intercultural communication in translation. In legal translation, legal knowledge is the knowledge of propositions of law in a narrow sense and the knowledge of legal culture in a broad sense, including legal systems, legal order, legal institutions, history, and practices and practitioners. (Salmi-Tolonen 2004: 1180-1181) Accordingly, the knowledge structures involved in legal translation comprise the specialized knowledge of law and the general knowledge of social-culture.

On one hand, the legal translator needs to acquire some specific knowledge of laws. There is a considerable disparity between the Anglo-American system of law and the systems in the civil law countries. Lack of legal knowledge may lead to misunderstanding that sometimes incurs absurd mistakes in legal translation. Take the term "civil prisoner" for example, it is ridiculous to translate it into a coined word "民事犯". Since the violation of civil law cannot be judged as a crime, the violator shouldn't be called a criminal（罪犯）at all. Actually, the "civil" here indicates that it is non-military, non-national or non-governmental. In other words, the crime committed by the "civil prisoner" constitutes no threat or damage to the interests of the army, the nation or the government. In this sense, it should be translated into "普通刑事犯" or "普通犯". (Chen 1998a: 109)

法律翻译
LEGAL TRANSLATION

The legal translator moving between two legal systems usually face the dilemma of absolute terminological asymmetry. However, the legal concepts, and the words in which those concepts are expressed, can usually be found and matched, as long as the legal translator are familiar with the two different systems. Therefore, the legal translator is required to "read between the lines" to draw out the correct content and legal effect, which implies that he/she should have some basic knowledge of legal systems and legal cultures.

On the other hand, an all-round knowledge background is essential for the legal translator, because the law touches upon almost every aspect of social life. Besides legal knowledge, the legal translator needs to be acquainted with many fields that law may deal with, such as business, patent and so on. A legal translator can't properly comprehend and reproduce a source text belonging to a discipline which is completely or partially strange to him/her. Translators also often acquire knowledge through translating. In addition, different cultural and historical backgrounds of different countries are usually reflected in their legal concepts and categories. Without an all-round knowledge of social-cultural background, it is impossible for the legal translator to perform well in translation tasks.

In a word, translational knowledge structures are extensive and diverse and vary from translator to translator. Legal translators need to possess general knowledge and specific knowledge of law to function as effective translators in this increasingly complex world.

Strategic Competence

Translation involves a processing and synthesizing ability, which is termed as translational strategic competence. More specifically, it refers to the special strategic skills that are employed in translational activities. In legal translation, translation strategies are crucial to the effectiveness in the communicative function of the translated texts. People may be highly proficient in two languages and sophisticated in knowledge structures (say, two legal systems and legal cultures),

Chapter Seven   Translation Competence and Techniques for Legal Translation

but this does not automatically make them effective legal translators without training or practice. There is a qualitative difference between knowing two languages and being a translator. For example, a bilingual lawyer do not become a proficient legal translator without training , but he/ she can acquire and develop his/ her legal translation skills.

It is generally believed that legal translators can make necessary alterations in lexis and syntax without affecting the substance of legal rules and common operation. In particular, legal translators are encouraged to be strategically competent, not for the sake of strategy itself, but to achieve the intended legal effects. Various strategies and methods can be used in the process of legal translation, and the translator has to decide which of the techniques is to be applied. Making reliable decisions requires not only legal competence but also considerable intuition on the part of legal translators. As for legal translation, intuition is not a natural ability but is acquired through interdisciplinary training in law and translation. Legal translators' strategic competence is visible through their strategies of dealing with legal translation, which will be shown in the following part.

Translation Techniques for Legal Translation

As we said previously, the legal translator needs to apply a dynamic treatment with multiple strategies. The translation process varies in terms of different legal texts, but generally it can be put into the following steps: having a thorough understanding of the source texts; deciding on what elements and functions need to be preserved; making a comparison of the equivalents available in target language; selecting a proper translation strategies and finally rendering a translation. In this part, several widely used strategies are illustrated in detail to help legal translators to perform their tasks well.

Translation Techniques on Lexical Level

Words are the building blocks of language. It is commonly acknowledged that one distinctive feature of legal language is the complex and unique legal vocabulary. The legal vocabulary in a language, including both legal concepts and legal usage, is extensive. Due to the systemic differences in law, many legal words in one language do not have equivalents in another, causing both linguistic and legal complications. Even so, legal texts can be translated from one language to another and from one legal system to another. In cases of no exact equivalence, the translator can select an alternative equivalent (i.e., the equivalent that most accurately conveys the legal sense of the source language and leads to the desired effects with multiply strategies).

Functional Equivalents

Legal vocabulary, especially legal terminology has peculiar legal meanings and effects, and cannot be changed at will. For some legal vocabulary, we can find direct correspondence in target legal system in terms of meaning and legal effect. In this case, legal translators are encouraged to use their counterparts rather than the neologism that may cause misunderstanding or even disputes on their interpretation. For example, the *incorporator* is translated into "公司组织者" in the book *English for the Legal Profession*. We cannot say this translation is wrong but it can be improved to some extent. There is a corresponding legal term "发起人" in China's *Company Law* adopted in 1993, thus it is better to follow it. (Zhu 2002: 68)

Of course, we can only search for functional equivalents in most cases. As defined by Sarcevic (1997: 278-279), functional equivalent is a term designating a concept or institution of the target legal system having the same function as a particular concept of the source legal system. That is to say, they are expected to lead to the same legal effect. However, there are some words in the source language

Chapter Seven   Translation Competence and Techniques for Legal Translation

that are linguistic equivalent to the source language, but may only carry partially equivalent meanings or sometimes may not be functionally equivalent in law at all. Take *jail* and *prison* for example, they are both translated into "监狱" in most dictionaries. Is it the true functional equivalent for both of them? According to *Oxford Dictionary of Practical Law*, a *jail* is a "building used for the confinement of individuals awaiting trail, or who have been convicted of minor offenses. The term PRISON is sometimes used interchangeably with *jail*, but PRISON is usually the place where only those with long term sentenced are confined." From this explanation, the meaning of *jail* and *prison* are slightly different. *Jail* is much closer to "看守所, 拘留所" in Chinese, while *prison* is equivalent with "监狱". Thus, the translator must also investigate the legal effect of the functional equivalent in the target legal system.

Lexical Expansion

A functional equivalent is inadequate when one or more of its essential characteristics differ from those of the source term in all or some contexts. In such cases, legal translators can sometimes compensate for the incongruency by using methods of lexical expansion to delimit or expand the sense of functional equivalent.

The translation of *barrister* and *solicitor* fully reflects the use of this technique. The distinction between *barrister* and *solicitor* is made only in British legal system. Essentially, *barristers* are the lawyers who represent litigants as their advocate before the courts of that jurisdiction. They speak in court and present the case before a judge or jury. In contrast, *solicitors* generally engage in preparatory work and advice, such as drafting and reviewing legal documents, dealing with and receiving instructions from the client, preparing evidence, and managing the day-to-day administration of a matter. There is no such division in China, so we only have the partial equivalent "律师". As a result, the former is translated into "巴律师", and the latter is translated into "沙律师" by means of transliteration, making

it correspond with a narrower functional equivalent.

It should be noted that lexical expansions are not natural functional equivalence because the concepts they denote do not exist in the target system. While some lexical expansions are acceptable, the legal translator is warned against going too far. If this method is not possible or would be too artificial, he/she should try other compensation strategies.

Descriptive Paraphrases

From the point of legal effect, paraphrasing is probably the most effective method of compensating for the lack of equivalence. That is to spell out the connotative meaning in ordinary language that can be understood by target receptors, thus enhancing the readability of the translated text. The translation of *yellow dog contract* is a typical example. If we translate it literally to "黄狗合同", it is difficult or even impossible for Chinese readers to get its real meaning because we do not have the concept of "黄狗合同" in Chinese laws. Actually, a yellow-dog contract is an agreement between an employer and an employee in which the employee agrees not to be a member of a labor union as a condition of employment. If we paraphrase its meaning "不准雇员参加工会的合同", it is more understandable for the Chinese readers.

Similarly, Prof. Chen Zhongcheng (1998a:103-106) also adopts the method of descriptive paraphrase when he attempts to translate the term *plea bargaining*. According to *Oxford Dictionary of Law*, it means "an agreement between the prosecution and the defence by which the accused changes his plea from not guilty to guilty in return for an offer by the prosecution (for example, to drop a more serious charge against the accused) or when the judge has informally let it be known that he will minimize the sentence if the accused pleads guilty." Upon understanding its definition and analyzing its application, Prof. Chen translates it into "关于（被告如何）认罪与（司法当局如何）处置的谈判". Here, *plea* is the plea of guilty made by the defence, and the prosecution also agrees to drop

Chapter Seven   Translation Competence and Techniques for Legal Translation

a more serious charge. This is a process whereby two sides negotiate a mutually satisfactory disposition of the case. Chen's translation is quite appropriate, combining the two aspects of *bargaining*.

For another example, "钓鱼执法" is a newly emerged legal vocabulary, which refers to a non-normal means, driven by financial interests, to induce law-abiding citizens to break the law, so as to conduct an economic punishment. By using paraphrase, it can be translated as: *For the financial interest, the law enforcement officials entrap law abiding citizens to break laws and impose a fine.*

Nonetheless, this technique is rarely used, probably because it distorts interlingual congruency. Besides, when paraphrasing a particular term, the legal translator actually plays a role as a drafter. Thus, he/she must have first-hand knowledge of the intent of the treaty-makers or contracting parties. As a note of caution, only the skilled translators with legal training are encouraged to attempt to use this method.

Neutral Terms

Akehurst (1972: 260) argues that the best solution when there is no adequate functional equivalent is to use neutral terms, i.e., non-technical terms. This is because neutral terms are usually broader in meaning than technical terms. The use of neutral terms is to have a meaning independent of target legal system to avoid misunderstanding. For instance, *deposition* is a legal term peculiar to Anglo-American procedural law. According to *Black's Law Dictionary*, it refers to a witness's out-of-court testimony that is reduced to writing (usu. by a court reporter) for later use in court or for discovery purposes. Since it is taken out of court, its literal translation "证词" is not accurate, which may create confusion with the *testimony* in Chinese legal system. Accordingly, Prof. Chen Zhongcheng (1998b: 143-145) recommends it be translated into "庭外采取的证词或供词的笔录".

For another example, both *libel* and *slander* are translated to "诽谤罪" by most legal translators. By definition, *slander* refers to a malicious, false, and

defamatory spoken statement or report, while *libel* refers to any other form of communication such as written words or images. In Anglo-American law system, *libel* and *slander* are tort law concepts rather than criminal law concepts, for the victim can file a claim for damages if there is an infringement of reputation. In China, the infringement are regulated by the civil law and criminal law respectively according to its severity. Obviously, *libel*, *slander* and "诽谤罪" are not equivalent legal concepts. Then, the neutral term "书面诽谤" for *libel* and "口头诽谤" for *slander* may avoid the confusion and serve the purpose well. (Chen 2004: 100)

Borrowing or Transliteration

Borrowing is the use of loanwords followed by footnotes, or supplementary information in parenthesis, thus making it clear that the word derives its meaning from the foreign legal system. With the increasingly frequent interaction with western countries, many English words are incorporated into Chinese language by borrowing, so are the legal terms. Before the reform and opening up, China's laws, especially laws and regulations in civil affairs, maritime affairs, environmental protection, marriage and family affairs, etc. are particularly weak. In order to improve China's socialist legal system, many foreign legal terms, such as "动产" (movable property), "收养" (adoption), "血亲" (cognation), etc. in Roman Law were introduced to China. The most typical is "法人" (legal person) in the civil law, which refers to "organizations with rights and enforcement capabilities, independently enjoying civil rights and assuming civil obligations, including enterprises and institutions, organs and social groups."

Borrowing can preserve the form and content of the original legal text as much as possible. It is sometimes the best way to achieve faithfulness without losing legal effect. *Money laundry*, for example, is translated into "洗钱" instead of "将违法所得及其产生的效益，通过各种手段掩饰、隐瞒其来源和性质，使其在形式上合法化的行为". This method reserves most of the original elements while the word order changes so as to ensure the correct syntactic arrangement in

Chapter Seven Translation Competence and Techniques for Legal Translation

Chinese. The detailed explanation of the exact meaning of the term can be provided in footnotes. Most frequently, however, the borrowing itself suffices to signalize the intended meaning.

Transliteration is another way to introduce new concepts and ideas. It is the act or process of representing or transcribing the words, letters or characters of one language into an alphabetic item of another language. In other words, transliteration indicates that the translated words are not native ones but the pronunciation of source language words written in the target language. Take the term *trust* for example, it is a common law institution that developed as a result of the historical separation of law and equity. The concept signifies a fiduciary relationship with respect to property, but there is no exact equivalent in Chinese legal system. Therefore, it is translated into "托拉斯" by the means of transliteration and thus *anti-trust law* is translated into "反托拉斯法". It should be noted that due to the large differences in pronunciation and semantic meanings between English and Chinese words, the transliterated words have to undergo "naturalized" treatment after entering the new legal contexts; that is, some slight changes in pronunciation or semantic meanings have to be made, to make them more close to the native words. In this case, *anti-trust law* is better translated as "反垄断法".

Borrowings or transliterations can be very useful when there are no satisfying equivalents available, but they should be grammatically acceptable and semantically transparent so as to enable the target users to grasp the general meaning of the source term.

Neologism

The concepts of English and Chinese legal terms are often unequal or even completely unequal. When the use of paraphrase, neutral and borrowed words in translation is unable to achieve functional equivalence, the corresponding neologisms should be created as new legal terms. For example, "婚内强奸" (marital rape) can be generated because feminists in western countries, such as Britain and

the United States, advocate the emancipation of women's personality. But this concept is not found in Chinese law.

The creation of neologism should follow the principle of monosemy, reflect the spirit of keeping pace with the times, and reveal the essential characteristics of the alleged legal things (phenomenon). We should pay attention to the aggregation and systematicness of semantics when creating the terms. For example, the legal term "成年人" (adult) appeared earlier in our legal system. The term *minor/infant* was originally translated as "青少年", "未成年人子女", etc., but is now generally translated as "未成年人" because this legal term is symmetrical with the semantic meaning of "成年人", so it's easy to understand and master, which embodies the systematic nature of legal terms and the dignity of law.

Translation Techniques on Syntactical Level

While legal vocabulary is the basis of legal texts, the translation never remains at the lexical level, but goes beyond. Words in legal translation never exist in isolation and their true meanings and legal effects cannot be fully appreciated unless they are construed with reference to the ways they are structured. For centuries, legal translators faithfully followed the syntax of the source text as closely as possible, mainly out of fear that any changes might disturb the thought process. This fear disappears when translators understand how legal rules operate and are able to express the intended logical relations. (Sarcevic 1997: 162) The following strategies are presented to illustrate how legal translators can make basic alterations in syntax without affecting the substance of legal rules and consequently their application. In particular, these adjustments are aimed at achieving dual equivalence in legal translation.

Repetition

Repetition is a technique frequently used in legal translation for it can make the rendered version clear in terms of meaning, and thus avoid ambiguity.

Chapter Seven Translation Competence and Techniques for Legal Translation

Example 1

The Company shall purchase other insurance policies at such time and in such amounts and with such times as deemed appropriate by the Board of Directors.

Chinese Version A: 在董事会认为合适的时候，合作公司还应购买其他保险，金额和条款也由董事会确定。

Chinese Version B: 合作公司应在董事会认为适当的时候以董事会认为适当的金额及董事会认为适当的条款购买其他保单。

Compared with Chinese Version A, Chinese Version B is clearer in terms of meaning. The word *shall* in the source text reigns over all the following elements in the sentence, the same as the Chinese word "应" in Chinese Version B. However, in Chinese Version A, the word "应" does not reign over all the elements in the sentence, with the elements "金额和条款也由董事会确定" left out or possibly left out. Under situations of this kind, repetition is employed in order to achieve clarity to the full extent.

Example 2

All permits, taxes and other fees arising from the prosecution and execution of the project shall be solely shouldered by the Contractor.

Chinese Version A: 项目施工过程中所产生的许可证费、税费及其他费用全部由承包方负担。

Chinese Version B: 项目执行、施工过程中所产生的许可证费、税费及其他费用均由承包方负担。

In Chinese Version A, *prosecution* and *execution* are translated into a single Chinese word "施工". But *prosecution* and *execution* are not exactly the same in terms of meaning. The source text, which uses them both rather than one, aims at making the meaning more complete and accurate. In the Chinese Version B, repetition is employed as in the source text.

Division of Long Sentences

As has been analyzed above, sentences in English legal texts are longer

and more complicated than in other text types, which can cause comprehension difficulty for the reader including the legal translator. It sometimes also makes the rendering into the Chinese language difficult. Legal translators therefore must choose between retaining the format (at the risk of incomprehensibility or added ambiguity) and undertaking vigorous breakdown of inconveniently long sentences into Chinese component parts prior to translation. Whichever course is taken, dual equivalence should be paramount for the translator.

When translating long and complex sentences, there are two basic steps: firstly, to conduct a careful analysis of the original sentence structure so as to comprehend the message; and secondly, to express and convey the meaning in the Chinese language. So, a good knowledge of syntactical rules of both languages is imperative. Sometimes, it may be necessary to break long sentences up and compose two or more sentences in the Chinese texts for the sake of readability, since the Chinese language tends to use several connected short sentences to express a concept or an action. Thus, division is a strategic method used in line with the features of Chinese sentence structure. For example,

> With respect to those territories to which this Convention is not extended at the time of signature, ratification or accession, each State concerned shall consider the possibility of taking the necessary steps in order to extend the application of this Convention to such territories, <u>subject, where necessary for constitutional reasons, to the consent of the Governments of such territories.</u>
>
> (Article X   *United Nations Convention on the Recognition and Enforcement of Foreign Arbitral Awards*)
>
> 关于在签署、批准或者参加本公约的时候，本公约所没有扩展到的地区，各有关国家应当考虑采取必要的步骤的可能性，以便本公约的适用范围能够扩展到这些地区。<u>但是，如果由于宪法关系而有必要时，应当取得这些地区的政府的同意。</u>
>
> 《联合国承认和执行外国仲裁裁决的公约》第十条

Chapter Seven   Translation Competence and Techniques for Legal Translation

The underlined part is an adverbial clause of condition led by "subject to," in which there is another conditional clause "where necessary for constitutional reasons." If the translator rendered the whole English sentence into one sentence in Chinese, it would be verbalized and bound to make the Chinese readers confused. By means of division, it is divided into two complete sentences in Chinese. The first sentence clearly conveys the core idea of the original sentence and the second one shows the restrictions. Hence, this kind of translation achieves the accurate and smooth effect in the light of the idiomatic Chinese expressions.

Adjustment of Word Order

The adjustment of word order is an important and useful technique employed in translating English legal texts. It is to change the linguistic order of the English sentences and restructure it according to the sequence of the Chinese language. The purpose of such adjustment is to make the translated version smooth for the Chinese readers to understand. There are two typical examples below:

(1) The borrower shall not do or cause or suffer anything to be done whereby the lender's interest may be prejudiced.

凡可导致贷款人的利益受损的事情，借款人均不得做出，或促使或容许其发生。

(2) Civil liability shall not be borne for failure to perform a contract or damage to a third party if it is caused by force majeure, except as otherwise provided by law.

因不可抗力不能履行合同或者造成他人损害的，不承担民事责任，法律另有规定的除外。

(*quoted from* Lu 2008: 69-70)

Example (1) is a restrictive attributive clause. If the translation kept the original sentence structure, it would be like "借款人不得做出或促使或容许任何事情发生借以使贷款人的利益可能受损". This version is awkward and difficult for

Chinese readers to understand for it is wordy and lacks clarity. It is better for the translator to exchange the position between the main clause and subordinate clause while translating it into Chinese in accordance with Chinese ways of expression.

Example (2) is a good example showing the different logical orders between English and Chinese. For the sake of emphasis, the most important part of a message is placed at the beginning of an English sentence while it is put at the end of the Chinese sentence. Since legal English is of hypotaxis and legal Chinese of parataxis, the translator makes a change of logical order between the two languages.

Transposition

Transposition means the substitution of one grammatical category for another on the basis that both may be fairly said to possess the same semantic weight. Transposition is a strategy frequently employed in legal translation. There are many kinds of transposition, such as transposition of part of speech, transposition of voice and transposition of sentence pattern.

A. Transposition of Part of Speech

Transposition of parts of speech is not uncommon in legal translation for this is an effective way to restructure the source text and avoid translationese. Almost all kinds of part of speech can be transposed in the translation between English and Chinese. Sometimes transposition is employed between the verb and the noun, sometimes between the adjective and the adverb. The transposition of part of speech mainly includes nouns, pronouns, prepositions, verbs, adjectives, adverbs and so on.

Example 1

The Parties agree that any restructuring shall not adversely affect the economic interests of the Parties.

Chinese Version: 双方同意，任何重组不得给双方的经济利益带来<u>不利的影响</u>。

In the Chinese version, the English adverb *adversely* is converted into the

Chapter Seven Translation Competence and Techniques for Legal Translation

Chinese adjective "不利的", whereas the English verb *affect* is converted into the Chinese noun "影响". If the strategy transposition is not employed here, the source sentence is very likely to be rendered into the Chinese version "双方同意，任何重组不得消极地影响双方的经济利益". The Chinese version using the strategy transposition concords to the linguistic habits of Chinese people and the one without using it sounds somewhat with the air of translationese.

Example 2

Unless otherwise provided for herein, <u>failure</u> or <u>delay</u> on the part of any party to exercise any right, power or privilege under this Agreement shall not operate as a <u>waiver</u> thereof, nor shall any <u>single</u> or <u>partial exercise</u> of any right, power or privilege preclude <u>further exercise</u> thereof or <u>exercise</u> of any other right, power or privilege.

除非本协议另有规定，任何一方<u>未能</u>或<u>延迟</u>行使其在本协议项下的任何权利、权力或特权，不应视为其<u>放弃</u>该权利、权力或特权；<u>单项或部分行使</u>任何权利、权力或特权，亦不妨碍其<u>进一步行使</u>该权利、权力或特权或<u>行使</u>其他权利、权力或特权。

In the process of translation, many parts of speech in the source text have been changed for the sake of clarity and preciseness. For example, the English noun *waiver* is transposed into the Chinese verb "放弃" and the English adjective *further* is rendered into the Chinese adverb "进一步". The underlined words in the source text have all undergone the shift of part of speech in the process of English to Chinese translation.

B. Transposition of Voice

For both English and Chinese, there is the classification of voice—active voice and passive voice. It is known that legal English is abundant in the use of the passive voice because the passive mood can be effective to suppress the identity of the agent responsible for the performance of the act. Compared with legal English, there are far less sentences of passive voice in legal Chinese. Accordingly, the legal translator, in most cases, should transform the passive voices in English legal

texts into active ones in Chinese version so as to produce more idiomatic Chinese sentences. This can be seen from the following examples.

Example 1

Confidential Information must be kept by the receiving Party in a secure place with access limited to only such Party's employees, contractors, or agents who need to know such information for the purposes of this Agreement and who have similarly agreed to keep such information confidential pursuant to a written confidentiality agreement which reflects the terms thereof.

收受方必须将机密信息保存在安全的地方,可以接触该等信息的人,仅限于该方为本协议之目的需要知道该等信息、且已按照一份反映本条条款的书面保密协议同样统一对该等信息进行保密的雇员、承包商或代理人。

Example 2

The Non-Disposing Party shall arrange the valuation, which shall be completed within three (3) months after the delivery of the Acceptance Notice.

非转让方应对评估做出安排,评估应在送交接受通知之日后三(3)个月内完成。

(*quoted from* Sun 2003: 192—193)

The above two examples are typical of converting English passive voice directly into Chinese active voice. However, it doesn't mean that all the passive voices in English need to be transformed into active voices in Chinese. The passive meanings can also be marked by auxiliary words such as "被" "受" "由" "为" "得到" "予以", etc. which are in essence equivalent to the passive voice. Examples are given below:

Example 3

Heads of federal departments are named by the President, and judges are either elected directly by the people or are appointed by elected officials.

Chapter Seven   Translation Competence and Techniques for Legal Translation

联邦政府各部部长部长<u>由总统任命</u>，法官<u>由人民直接选举</u>，或者<u>由选举出来的官员任命</u>。

Example 4

If the dispute <u>cannot be resolved by negotiations</u> within thirty (30) days after one Party has issued notice to the other Party requesting the commencement of such negotiations, then either Party may submit it to the Singapore International Arbitration Center for arbitration in accordance with the UNCITRAL rules of arbitration.

如果在一方向另一方发出要求就争议开始进行谈判的书面通知后三十（30）日内，<u>争议未能得到解决</u>，则任何一方均可将争议提交新加坡国际仲裁中心，由仲裁机构根据联合国际贸易法委员会的仲裁规则进行仲裁。

(*quoted from* Sun 2003: 191-192)

C. Transposition of Negation

Legal English is featured by the frequent occurrence of negative forms. The negative forms of legal English often find expression in the words such as *not, never, no, deny* and so on. Sometimes they will be reflected in the words with the prefix such as "mis-" and "un-" or the suffix "-less." It is not rare to encounter double negation, triple negation or even quadruple negation in legal English. In Chinese, there are negative forms as well. But there is a major difference between them: In English, the subject of a sentence is more likely to be negated, whereas in Chinese, it is more likely to negate the predicate. Thus, in the process of English-Chinese legal translation, transposition of negation is sometimes encountered.

Example 1

<u>No party</u> shall issue or make any public announcement or disclose any information regarding this agreement.

任何一方均<u>不得</u>发布、公开、披露与本协议有关的任何信息。

109

Example 2

No terms or provisions of this Agreement shall be varied or modified by any prior or subsequent statement, conduct or act of either of the Parties, except that the Parties may amend this Agreement by written instruments referring to and executed in the same manner as this Agreement.

任何一方均不得以先前或以后的声明、行动或行为变更或修改本协议的任何条款或规定,但双方可以以本协议提及的和以本协议相同方式执行的书面文件修正本协议。

In the two examples listed above, transposition of negation takes place in the process of E-C translation. Their subjects are negated in the source text, but the negation is shifted to the predicates in the target text.

Chapter Eight

Translation on the Programmed Structures in Legal Texts

Strategies for Translating Fuzzy Expression

The successful legal translation not only requires the translator to master the meaning of words and sentences in the original text, but also requires the translator to have a comprehensive understanding of the effect of the original text so as to get the same effect in the target language. Based on Nida and Newmark's theory, when translating fuzzy expressions into another language, translators can produce corresponding fuzzy expressions in the target language, i.e., fuzziness to fuzziness translation strategy.

This part tentatively introduces four strategies for translating fuzzy expressions in legislative language: equivalence, converting, adding and omitting.

Equivalence

Equivalence means to translate fuzzy expressions in the source language into corresponding fuzzy expressions in the target language, i.e., fuzziness to fuzziness.

The equivalence here means the pursuit of the closest degree in fuzziness instead of absolute sameness. To some degree, this method can also be called the literal translation. As a possible and in many cases a desirable approach in handling fuzziness in source language, it is frequently adopted, especially when the lawmakers intentionally employ fuzzy expressions in the legislative process.

Example 1

故意毁坏公私财物，数额<u>较大</u>或者有其他<u>严重</u>情节的，处三年以下有期徒刑、拘役或者罚金；数额<u>巨大</u>或者有其他<u>特别严重</u>情节的，处三年以上七年以下有期徒刑。

——《中华人民共和国刑法》，第二百七十五条

Whoever intentionally destroys or damages public or private money or property, if the amount involved is <u>relatively large</u> or if there are other <u>serious</u> circumstances, shall be sentenced to fixed-term imprisonment of not more than three years, or criminal detention or be fined; if the amount involved is <u>huge</u>, or if there are other <u>especially serious</u> circumstances, he shall be sentenced to fixed-term imprisonment of not less than three years but not more than seven years.

— Article 275 *Criminal Law of the People's Republic of China*

Example 2

中华人民共和国保护华侨的<u>正当</u>的权利和利益，保护归侨和侨眷的<u>合法</u>的权利和利益。

——《中华人民共和国宪法》，第五十条

The People's Republic of China protects the <u>legitimate</u> rights and interests of Chinese nationals residing abroad and protects the <u>lawful</u> rights and interests of returned overseas Chinese and of the family members of Chinese nationals residing abroad.

— Article 50 *Constitution of the People's Republic of China*

Example 3

现役军人的配偶要求离婚，须得军人同意，但军人一方有<u>重大</u>过错的除外。

——《中华人民共和国婚姻法》，第三十三条

Chapter Eight Translation on the Programmed Structures in Legal Texts

If the spouse of a soldier in active service desires a divorce, the matter shall be subject to the soldier's consent, unless the soldier has made <u>grave</u> errors.

— Article 33 *Marriage Law of the People's Republic of China*

Example 4

当事人一方违约后，对方应当采取<u>适当</u>措施防止损失的扩大；没有采取<u>适当</u>措施致使损失扩大的，不得就扩大的损失要求赔偿。

当事人因防止损失扩大而支出的<u>合理</u>费用，由违约方承担。

—《中华人民共和国合同法》，第一百一十九条

After either party breaches the contract, the other party shall take <u>appropriate</u> measures to prevent the increase of the loss; the party that fails to take <u>appropriate</u> preventive measures and thus aggravates the loss may not claim compensation for the increased part of the loss.

The <u>reasonable</u> expenses incurred by the other party in preventing the aggravation of the loss shall be borne by the breaching party.

— Article 119 *Contract Law of the People's Republic of China*

Example 5

赠与人的经济状况<u>显著</u>恶化，<u>严重</u>影响其生产经营或者家庭生活的，可以不再履行赠与义务。

—《中华人民共和国合同法》，第一百九十五条

A donor whose financial conditions deteriorate <u>markedly</u> and whose production, business or family life is thereby <u>severely</u> affected may cease to perform the donation obligations.

— Article 195 *Contract Law of the People's Republic of China*

Example 6

……业主大会和业主委员会，对任意弃置垃圾、排放污染物或者噪声、违反规定饲养动物、违章搭建、侵占通道、拒付物业费等损害他人合法权益的行为，有权依照法律、法规以及管理规约，要求行为人停止<u>侵</u>害、消除<u>危险</u>、排除<u>妨</u>害、赔偿<u>损</u>失。……

—《中华人民共和国物权法》，第八十三条

...With respect to a person who randomly discards garbage, discharges pollutants, makes noises, keeps animals in violation of regulations, erects structures against rules, occupies passages, refuses to pay property management fees, etc. , thus infringing on the lawful rights and interests of another person, the owners' assembly and the owners' committee shall, according to the relevant laws and regulations and the management rules and agreements, have the right to require the person to discontinue such <u>infringement</u>, eliminate the <u>hazards</u>, clear away the <u>obstructions</u> and compensate the <u>losses</u> entailed. ...

—Article 83 *Property Law of the People's Republic of China*

Example 7

进出境的样品、礼品、暂准进出境的货物以及<u>其他非贸易性物品</u>，免予检验。但是，法律、行政法规另有规定的除外。……

—《中华人民共和国进出口商品检验法实施条例》，第六条

Product samples, gifts, goods admitted temporarily and <u>other nontrade articles</u> that enter or exit the territory are exempted from inspection, unless otherwise provided by laws or administrative regulations. ...

—Article 6 *Regulations on Implementation of the Law of the People's Republic of China on Import and Export Commodity Inspection*

Example 8

夫妻双方都有参加生产、工作、学习和社会活动的自由，一方不得对他方加以<u>限制</u>或<u>干涉</u>。

—《中华人民共和国婚姻法》，第十五条

Both husband and wife shall have the freedom to engage in production and other work, to study and to participate in social activities; neither party shall <u>restrict</u> or <u>interfere</u> with the other party.

— Article 15 *Marriage Law of the People's Republic of China*

The above-mentioned examples all employ the method of equivalence or literal translation, using fuzzy counterparts in the target language and Chinese expressions are faithfully translated. We can see that in some cases the existence of

Chapter Eight Translation on the Programmed Structures in Legal Texts

certain fuzzy expressions can determine whether a behavior is a crime or not and ensure that the punishment fits the crime. Therefore, the legal translator should treat them carefully in the process of translation.

Converting

Converting is a quite common method of translation due to language differences. It includes the conversion of part of speech, sentence structure, tense, voice, mood, etc. The translator should get a full understanding of the semantic structure in the source language, and make flexible conversion when necessary.

Converting Part of Speech
Example 1
夫妻应当互相忠实，互相尊重；家庭成员间应当敬老爱幼，互相帮助，维护平等、和睦、文明的婚姻家庭关系。

——《中华人民共和国婚姻法》，第四条

Husband and wife shall be loyal to each other and respect each other; family members shall respect the old and cherish the young, help each other, and maintain the marriage and family relationship characterized by equality, harmony and civility.

— Article 4 *Marriage Law of the People's Republic of China*

The Chinese "平等的""和睦的""文明的" are fuzzy expressions. What kind of family relationship can be described to be equal, harmonious and civilized? There is no clear boundary. In this example, nominalization makes the expressions concisely convey the fuzzy meaning denoted in the original. The use of noun forms in the target language also makes the expression more formal, which is one of the principal features of the legislative language.

Converting Fuzzy Phrases into Sentences
Sometimes the fuzzy adjectives in Chinese can not be translated into the same fuzzy adjectives in English. The translator should change the adjectives in

the original text into a clause. The following examples illustrate how the translator renders the fuzzy phrases in Chinese into a English sentence which still conveys the original meaning.

Example 2

……本法所称不可抗力,是指<u>不能预见</u>、<u>不能避免并不能克服的客观情况</u>。

—《中华人民共和国合同法》,第一百一十七条

…Force majeure as used herein means objective situations <u>which cannot be foreseen, avoided or overcome</u>.

—Article 117 *Contract Law of the People's Republic of China*

Example 3

……(二)国境口岸有关部门应当采取切实可行的措施,控制啮齿动物、病媒昆虫,使其数量降低<u>到不足为害的程度</u>。

—《中华人民共和国国境卫生检疫法实施细则》,第一百零五条

…(2) the units concerned at the border port are required to take effective measures to minimize the number of rodents or vector pests <u>so they may not cause any harm</u>.

— Article 105 *Rules for the Implementation of the Frontier Health and Quarantine Law of the People's Republic of China*

Adding

Chinese and English are two totally different languages. They belong to different language systems, and both of them have their own distinctive features in language structure, idiomatic expressions, etc.

When a Chinese sentence is translated into English, adding some words can show some implied messages not denoted in the source text, making the meaning more specific and the target text more readable. Besides, the adding part may be an important part of a sentence in the target language.

Chapter Eight　Translation on the Programmed Structures in Legal Texts

Adding the Conceptual Information

Example 1

广告使用数据、统计资料、调查结果、文摘、引用语等引证内容的，应当<u>真实</u>、准确，并表明出处。

—《中华人民共和国广告法》，第十一条

Data, statistical information, results of investigation or survey, digest quotations and other citations used in an advertisement shall <u>be true to facts</u> and accurate, and their sources shall be indicted.

—Article 11 *Advertisement Law of the People's Republic of China*

Example 2

……禁止重婚。禁止有配偶者与<u>他人</u>同居。……

—《中华人民共和国婚姻法》，第三条

…Bigamy shall be prohibited. Anyone who has a spouse shall be prohibited to cohabit with <u>another person of the opposite sex</u>. …

—Article 3 *Marriage Law of the People's Republic of China*

In example 1, the word "真实" contains fuzzy meaning, so the translator translated it into "be true to facts" to make the meaning more precise and complete. In example 2, "他人" is a fuzzy noun. The meaning "of the opposite sex," which is connoted but not denoted in the original text, were added in the translation to make the translation more precise.

Adding the Structural Information

Example 3

侮辱、殴打教师的，根据不同情况，分别给予行政处分或者行政处罚；造成损害的，责令赔偿损失；情节严重，构成犯罪的，依法追究刑事责任。

—《中华人民共和国教师法》，第三十五条

Anyone who insults or assaults a teacher shall be given an administrative sanction or penalty depending on the different circumstances; those who have caused losses

or injury shall be ordered to compensate for the losses; and if the circumstances are serious enough to constitute a crime, the offender shall be investigated for criminal responsibility according to law.

—Article 35 *Teachers Law of the People's Republic of China*

In this example, the word "严重" is used to make a comparison with the above-mentioned situations, and in the original text, the seriousness is also qualified as "构成犯罪的", so this part should be translated as "serious enough to constitute a crime." "Enough" should be added to make the meaning of the sentence more complete.

Adding the Background Information
Example 4
凡在中华人民共和国领域内犯罪的，除法律有特别规定的以外，都适用本法。……

—《中华人民共和国刑法》，第六条

This Law shall be applicable to anyone who commits a crime within the territory and territorial waters and space of the People's Republic of China, except as otherwise specifically provided by law.

— Article 6 *Criminal Law of the People's Republic of China*

Translators are encouraged to compensate for the information lost in translation. In this example, we Chinese know that "领域" includes not only "territory" but also "territorial waters and space," but this kind of information should be conveyed to the target audience so as to avoid loopholes.

Omitting

Omitting helps reduce some irrelevant, trivial or redundant information, which can be implied in the targeted language, to make the translation more concise and smooth.

Chapter Eight   Translation on the Programmed Structures in Legal Texts

Example

……海关查问违法嫌疑人或者询问证人应当制作笔录，并当场交其辨认，没有异议的，立即签字确认；有异议的，予以更正后签字确认。

——《中华人民共和国海关行政处罚实施条例》，第四十三条

...When interrogating a person suspected of violating the law or questioning a witness, the Customs shall take a record thereof and show him such record on the spot for him to identify. If there is no dissent, such record shall be confirmed with signature; if any dissent arises, such record shall be corrected and confirmed with signature.

—Article 43 *Regulations of the People's Republic of China on Implementing Customs Administrative Penalty*

In this example, "立即" is connoted in the target text. In order to avoid translationese and make the translation smooth, the translator should resort to the translation approach of omitting to make the translation idiomatic.

Summary

The first translation method can be seen as literal translation, which is to find the corresponding fuzzy expressions in the target language. In most cases, the translator can easily find the appropriate counterparts in the target language. The other three methods can be viewed as, to some extent, free translation, which is defined as a translation conveying the meaning and spirit of the SL without sticking to the original form. In a word, translators may employ different techniques to translate fuzzy expressions.

Strategies for Translating Sentences with "的" Structure

As a major issue and difficulty in the translation of the project, "的" structure

has appeared frequently in legislative texts. In this part, solutions for translating the sentences with " 的 " structure in legislative texts will be examined.

As an Adverbial Clause of Condition

Since the "的" structure in Chinese legislative texts is usually used to indicate a condition, it is reasonable to translate it into English as an adverbial clause of condition correspondingly. "Generally speaking, adverbial clause in legal texts is introduced by 'if', 'where', 'when', 'in case', 'in the event that', 'should', 'provided', 'providing' and so forth" (Li 2008: 72).

According to Li Kexing (2008), a conditional clause introduced by "if" implies an event or a situation that is probably to happen. There are few differences between "if" and "where" when they function as an introducer of an adverbial clause of condition in legal English, while the latter is more formal in terms of stylistic feature. On the other hand, a clause that is introduced by "in case" or "in the event that" implies a situation that is not likely to happen. In this sense, "if" and "where" can be used interchangeably. Nevertheless, in accordance with the principle of consistence and identity, one word must be chosen. In the translation project, "where" was chosen as the introducer of conditional clause.

Example 1
代理人违反第二款规定的，劳动人事争议仲裁委员会可以取消其代理资格。
——《江苏省劳动人事争议调解仲裁办法》第三十条
Where any agent violates the provisions of the second paragraph, the labor and personnel dispute arbitration commission may dismiss his qualification of agency.
— Article 30 *Measures of Jiangsu Province on Mediation and Arbitration of Labor and Personnel Disputes*

Example 2
当事人主张仲裁时效中断、中止的，应当对其主张承担举证责任。
——《江苏省劳动人事争议调解仲裁办法》第三十六条
Where either party proposes interruption or suspension of arbitration period,

Chapter Eight Translation on the Programmed Structures in Legal Texts

the party shall bear the burden of proof.

— Article 36 *Measures of Jiangsu Province on Mediation and Arbitration of Labor and Personnel Disputes*

There are a lot of articles, like those cited above, with the "的" structure in the source text. In this case, although there is no sign of conditional clause such as "如果" or "若" in the source texts, it can be indentified that the "的" structure implies an assumption which is the prerequisite of the legal action.

As a Non-finite verb

"有下列情形之一的" is one of the common expressions in Chinese legislative texts used to list situations or behaviors that meet some specific legal provisions or that bear the same legal liability. (Zou 2008: 101) Generally, it is translated into "under one of the following circumstances" in a legislative text. The matters following this expression is usually written in "的" structure. In this case, it tends to be rendered as non-finite verb, as is shown in the following example.

Example

仲裁决定适用于下列事项：

（一）对管辖权有异议的；

（二）是否需要回避的；

（三）中止、终结或者恢复审理的；

（四）撤销不予受理通知或者案件的；

……

——《江苏省劳动人事争议调解仲裁办法》第四十一条

Arbitration decisions shall apply to the following matters:

1. <u>Having</u> objections to jurisdiction;

2. Whether there is a need for withdrawal;

3. <u>Suspending</u> and <u>completing</u> or <u>resuming</u> trial;

4. <u>Revoking</u> not-to-accept notices or cases;

—— Article 41 *Measures of Jiangsu Province on Mediation and Arbitration of Labor and Personnel Disputes*

To Complement the Subject

It is known that parataxis is one of the syntactical features of Chinese language, while hypotaxis is that of English. In a Chinese sentence, various parts of speech can be used as the subject and some sentences have no subject at all, which are called zero-subject sentences. According to Chen and Li (2010: 41), Chinese is a topic-prominent language, while English is a subject-prominent language. As a result, in Chinese-English translation practice, the key of a good translation lies in defining the subject and the predicate.

Actually,"的" structure in Chinese is a syntactic structure in which the logic subject is omitted. (Dong 2011: 158) Consequently, translating this kind of zero-subject sentence, one may complement the subject in accordance with the context.

Example 1

仲裁员有下列情形之一的，应当回避，当事人也有权提出回避申请：

（一）是本案的当事人或者当事人、代理人近亲属的；

（二）与本案有利害关系的；

……

——《江苏省劳动人事争议调解仲裁办法》第三十八条

An arbitrator shall withdraw, and the parties also have the right to apply for withdrawal, under one of the following circumstances:

(1) He is a party to the case or a close relative of a party or its agent;

(2) He has an interest in the case;

…

—— Article 38 *Measures of Jiangsu Province on Mediation and Arbitration of Labor and Personnel Disputes*

Chapter Eight Translation on the Programmed Structures in Legal Texts

Example 2

因正当防卫造成损害的，不承担民事责任。

——《中华人民共和国民法总则》第一百八十一条

A person who causes harm in exercising justifiable defense shall not bear civil liability.

— Article 181 *General Provisions of the Civil Law of the People's Republic of China*

In the source text of Example 1, the qualifications listed in the sub-clause, such as "是本案的当事人或者当事人、代理人近亲属的", are not complete sentences but they are nominalized by "的" structure. Having been nominalized, the sentences have the function of transferred-designation. They refer to the person who meets the qualification. Although the subject is omitted, it can be identified from the context which refers to the "仲裁员". In this case, the subject should be complemented so as to conform to the English syntactic structure. When it comes to the zero-subject sentence in Example 2, the logical subject should also be added.

Translation of Some Typical Expressions

Where

In common English, adverbial clauses led by "where" usually indicate the location, while in legal English, "where" in clauses is identical to "in the case where" and the most typical translation of it is "如果/如……" "当/在……时" or "的" structure.

Example 1

Where a restraining order has been revoked or varied under this section, notice of such revocation or the order as so varied, as the case may be, shall be served on the third party to whom it is directed and on the suspected person.

Translation: 凡限制令已根据本条被撤销或更改，无论撤销或更改，该项决定的通知书应送达限制令所针对的第三人和犯罪嫌疑人。

Example 2

Where an employee is granted any period of annual leave, the employer shall pay him annual leave pay in respect of that period not later than the day on which he is next paid his wages after that period.

Translation: 雇员获准休年假的，雇主应于不迟于该年假后第一个发薪日，支付该雇员该段年假的薪酬。

Example 3

Where a defendant is fined and the same is not forthwith paid, the magistrate may order the defendant to be searched.

Translation: 对被告罚款后，被告未能立即缴付的，治安法官可裁定对被告搜身。

Example 4

Where a claimant has a claim which exceeds the monetary amount mentioned in the Schedule and which, but for the excess, would be within the jurisdiction of the Board, the claimant may abandon the excess, and thereupon the Board shall have jurisdiction to inquire into, hear and determine the claim.

Translation: 若申请人申请的标的数额超过附录中的数额，且除去超出部分后的数额属仲裁处管辖的，申请人可以放弃超出部分。因此，仲裁处有权对案件进行调查、听证并裁决。

Subject to

"Subject to" is often translated into "以……为条件" "根据……规定" "在符合……的情况下" "除……另有规定外" "在不抵触……下", etc. in legal texts.

Example 1

Subject to subsection (4), the information referred to in section 13(2) and in section 14(2) may be required from a legal adviser as from any other person,

Chapter Eight   Translation on the Programmed Structures in Legal Texts

notwithstanding that the effect of compliance with such a requirement would be to disclose any privileged information or communication.

Translation: 在符合第 4 款规定的情况下，可以要求法律顾问提供第 13(2) 和第 14(2) 条提及的信息，就如同要求任何人提供该类信息一样，尽管法律顾问遵照该类要求的结果可能会披露特许信息或交流内容。

Example 2

Subject to subsection (3), the Board shall have jurisdiction to inquire into, hear and determine the claims specified in the Schedule.

Translation: 在不违反第 (3) 款规定的情况下，仲裁处有权调查、审理并裁决附表中所列的各类仲裁案件。

Example 3

Subject to the provisions of subsections (2) and (3), where a term of imprisonment is imposed by a magistrate in respect of the non-payment of an sum of money adjudged to be paid by a conviction or order, that term shall, on payment of a part of such sum to any person authorized by a magistrate to receive it, be reduced by a number of days bearing as nearly as possible the same proportion to the total number of days in the term as the sum paid bears to the sum adjudged to be paid.

Translation: 在符合第 (2) 和 (3) 款规定的情况下，若罪犯因不履行判决或裁定判定应付的款项，而被治安法官判处有期徒刑，该刑期在罪犯将部分款项缴付治安法官授权的接收人后，可按缴付款项所占应缴数额的比例，尽可能准确地按照同样比例减少刑期。

Provided that

"Provided that" is an old expression which is rarely used in common English, while it is widely used in legal English (especially in contracts, agreements and articles). If it is placed at the beginning of the sentence and followed by a conditional clause, it is equivalent to "if" or "where," which means "倘若/如果" in

Chinese. If it is put after a matrix clause, the clauses led by "provided that" indicate the opposite conditions of the one mentioned before, which is identical to "with the exception of" and can be translated into "但" or "但是".

Example 1

Contributions to the registered capital of the Company shall be made by the parties in accordance with Schedule 1; provided however that schedule 1 may be adjusted by the unanimous vote of the Board in light of actual conditions consistent with the requirements of relevant regulations and provided further that the obligation of any Party to make its initial contribution shall be subject to the fulfillment or waiver of each of the following conditions.

Translation: 双方应依照附录1向合营公司的注册资本出资；但是，根据实际条件并在符合有关法规的情况并且每一方完成其首期出资的义务取决于下列每项条件均已得到满足或均已被放弃。

Example 2

Provided that the documentation is found incomplete or unclear Party A shall notify Party B in time. Party B shall make timely improvements in order to solve the problem.

Translation: 如果发现资料不全、不清楚，甲方将及时通知乙方，乙方将及时改进，以解决问题。

Example 3

Either party may at any time replace the chairman, deputy chairman or director it has appointed provided that it gives written notice to the Joint Venture Company and the other party.

Translation: 任何一方可以随时更换自己委派的董事长、副董事长或董事，但必须书面通知合营公司和合营他方。

For the Purpose(s) of

In legal English, "for the purpose of…" often appears in the general provisions

Chapter Eight   Translation on the Programmed Structures in Legal Texts

of laws and regulations. If it is followed by a specific chapter, article, section, subsection, etc., "for the purpose of…" can be translated into "就某章、节、条、款、项、目而言" "对……来说" "为了实施该(条法例)". Otherwise, it can be replaced by "for," "in order to," "with a view to" and be translated into "为了……".

Example 1

For the purpose of these presents any act default or omission of the agents, servants, workmen or licensees of the Tenant shall be deemed to be the act, default or omission of the Tenant.

Translation: 本文件中，租户的代理人、佣人、工人或受许可人的任何行为、过错或不作为，应被认为是租户的行为、过错或不作为。

Example 2

For the purposes of subsection (2), "land" does not include incorporeal hereditament.

Translation: 第二款所称土地，不包括可继承无形资产。

Example 3

For the purposes of subsection (3) permission shall be in writing and…

Translation: 第三款所称许可，应采用书面形式……

Example 4

本法所称的发明创造是指发明、实用新型和外观设计。

——《中华人民共和国专利法》第二条

Translation: For the purpose of this Law, "invention-creation" means inventions, utility models and designs.

—Article 2 *Patent Law of the People's Republic of China*

Example 5

A judge may, on the application of an appellant who is in custody, order the appellant to be brought up to the court in custody for the purpose of attending his appeal or any application or any proceeding therein.

Translation: 应受羁押的上诉人的申请，法官可裁定将上诉人在羁押下带上法庭，以出庭参加上诉、申请之事或任何程序。

Example 6

为了促进和保障苏南国家自主创新示范区建设,加快提升自主创新能力,发挥示范和辐射带动作用,根据有关法律、行政法规,结合实际,制定本条例。

——《苏南国家自主创新示范区条例》,第一条

Translation: These regulations are formulated in accordance with relevant laws and administrative regulations, in light of the specific situation, and for the purpose of promoting and safeguarding the construction of the Sunan National Innovation Park, accelerating the upgrading of independent innovation capability and putting into play its role as a demonstration and driving force.

— Article 1 *Regulations on the Sunan National Innovation Park*

Chapter Nine

Translation on Marketing Agreements

Introduction

Types of Marketing Agreements

There are various types of marketing agreements, including:
- Agency agreements
- Distribution agreements
- Franchising agreements
- Joint venture agreements

Agency Agreement

A traditional sales agency agreement is an agreement whereby a company (known as the principal) authorises another company or individual (known as the agent) to sell the principal's goods on its behalf. The agent thus sells the goods on behalf of the principal (rather than purchase the goods itself). When a customer purchases from the agent the contractual relationship (known as "privity of contract") will thereby legally exist directly between the principal and the purchaser (the agent receiving commission on such sales).

Distribution Agreement

This is an agreement whereby a company (termed the supplier) actually sells its goods to another company (the distributor). When the distributor then sells the goods to its own customer, there is no contract created between the supplier and the final customer (the contract being between the distributor and its customer). The distributor therefore receives no commission from the supplier, instead earning profit from the "mark-up" between the price it paid the supplier and the price it sold the goods on for.

Franchise Agreement

A company (the franchisor) can expand its business nationally and internationally by entering into franchise agreements with other parties (known as franchisees). This is known as franchising a business. Franchising is appropriate to businesses with an established brand. A franchise agreement imposes requirements on the franchisee to operate the business in accordance with a uniform business model (for instance by stipulating the colour scheme and interior layout of the franchisee's premises). The franchisee benefits, however, by being associated with a well recognized brand-name. Many well-known high street brands are franchises, such as fast-food restaurants.

Joint Venture Agreement

This is an arrangement in which two or more businesses agree to co-operate or in other words "join forces" on a particular business venture or project. This enables companies to undertake initiatives which they may not have the resources to undertake individually, sharing risks while also combining their financial resources and skills.

Drafting Agreements

Drafting is an important skill. Drafting in the legal sense means to compose legal documentation (including for instance legal correspondence, court orders,

Chapter Nine   Translation on Marketing Agreements

contracts and legislation). Precision is essential when drafting legal agreements; otherwise there may be scope for ambiguity in the course of interpreting the intended meaning of the terms of the agreement. This in turn can lead to subsequent dispute between the parties to the agreement. Drafting practice provides the opportunity to develop your skill in the use of legal English.

The following agreement relates to the appointment of an agent by an aircraft manufacturer called Cadmium Aerospace Limited.

AGENCY AGREEMENT

THIS AGREEMENT is made on the 19th day of July 2007

BETWEEN:

(1) CADMIUM AEROSPACE LIMITED, whose registered office is at 168 Hanover Square, London, W1 ("the Principal")

AND

(2) MACFADYEN AVIATION LIMITED, whose registered office is at 115 Duxford Road, Cambridge, CM3 ("the Agent").

1. APPOINTMENT

The Principal hereby appoints the Agent and the Agent agrees to act as the Agent of the Principal for the purpose of promoting and selling the Principal's aircraft throughout Europe and North America ("the Territory"). It is further agreed that this agreement shall be valid for a period of two years. Moreover, the Principal agrees not to appoint any other agent in the territory and furthermore agrees not to seek nor enter into sales itself within the Territory during the period of the Agreement.

2. AGENT'S OBLIGATIONS

2.1 The Agent hereby undertakes to use its best endeavours to market and achieve sales of the Principal's aircraft in the Territory. The Agent is also henceforth authorised to enter into contracts for the sale of the Principal's aircraft for and on behalf of the Principal.

2.2 In addition, the Agent undertakes to provide the Principal with market reports on monthly sales and competitors' activities.

2.3 The Agent shall make appropriate credit checks on potential customers in order to ensure their credit-worthiness.

3. PRINCIPAL'S OBLIGATIONS

3.1 The Principal hereby agrees that during the continuance of the Agreement it will:

3.1.1 provide the Agent with training on the Principal's aircraft;

3.1.2 provide customers with technical and servicing report;

3.1.3 provide the Agent with marketing and publicity material to assist the Agent with marketing the Principal's aircraft within the Territory.

4. REMUNERATION

4.1 The Agent shall receive from the Principal in consideration of its services hereunder commission as follows:

4.1.1 at a rate of 5% of the Net Selling Price for each single engined "Strato-Line" airplane sold;

4.1.2 at a rate of 7% of the Net Selling Price for each twin engined "Skymaster" airplane sold.

EXECUTED BY   (Sales Director)

For and on behalf of CADMIUM AEROSPACE LIMITED

EXECUTED BY   (Chief Executive Officer)

For and on behalf of MACFADYEN AVIATION LIMITED

Chapter Nine Translation on Marketing Agreements

Law Notes

Marketing Agreements

Agency Agreement

◆ Agent sells goods or services on behalf of a principal, the principal selling directly to the final customer.

◆ Privity of contract exists between the principal and the ultimate purchaser

◆ Agent receives commission

◆ Agency agreements are often more suitable for high-value items such as aero-engines etc.

◆ Agent's duties include:

1. promoting the goods or services in the market place
2. providing principal with feedback information on sales and market trends
3. maintaining confidentiality regarding principal's trade secrets

◆ Principal's duties involve acting in good faith towards the agent and usually include:

1. paying commission
2. supplying advertising and promotional literature
3. supplying stock as required and after-sales service

Distribution Agreement

◆ Supplier sells to a distributor in a particular market (often in another country), no contract existing between the supplier and the final customer

◆ Distributor earns income from "mark-up" between price paid to supplier for goods and selling price to customer

◆ Distributor's duties usually include:

1. purchasing a specified minimum amount of stock from the supplier on a

regular basis

2. marketing and promoting effectively goods purchased from the supplier and keeping supplier informed of sales levels and market trends

3. ensuring that similar competitors' products are not sold or promoted

◆ Supplier's duties usually include:

1. providing advertising and sales promotional material

2. selling a specified amount of stock regularly to the distributor

3. indemnifying the distributor from any legal liability resulting from any defect in the products

Franchising Agreement

A contractual arrangement in which a franchisor appoints a franchisee to operate as a separate business offering the franchisor's goods or services. The franchisee usually pays a franchise fee as well as possibly a continuing royalty fee on sales. In return the franchisee benefits from a recognized "brand-image."

Joint Venture Agreement

An agreement whereby two or more separate businesses co-operate with each other on a particular commercial venture or project. Such an agreement enables the separate businesses to combine resources and to share financial risk for mutual benefit.

Expressions Commonly Used in Marketing Agreements

● **Whereas:** considering that 鉴于，就……而论（法律用语）

Example 1

Whereas Party A is willing to employ Party B and Party B agrees to act as

Chapter Nine   Translation on Marketing Agreements

Party A's Engineer in Bamako, it is hereby mutually agreed as follows:

鉴于甲方愿意聘请乙方，乙方同意应聘为甲方在巴马科（工程）的工程师，合同双方特此达成协议如下：

Example 2

Whereas Party B and Party A have entered into this Contract to install Party A's air-conditioning equipment, the Parties hereto do hereby agree as follows:

鉴于乙方与甲方订立本合同，安装甲方的空气调节设备，双方同意如下：

● **In Witness Whereof:** 特此立（证）据，以此立（证）据等

● **In Testimony Whereof:** 以此为证，特立此证

● **Whereby:** by the agreement; by the following terms and conditions, etc. 凭此协议，凭此条款等

Example 1

In Witness Whereof the Parties hereto have caused this Agreement to be executed on the day and year first before written in accordance with their respective laws.

本协议书由双方根据各自的法律签订，于上面所签订的日期开始执行，特立此据。

Example 2

In Testimony Whereof, we have hereto signed this document on _____ (day/month/year).

我方于_____年_____月_____日签署本文，特此证明。

Example 3

A sales contract refers to a contract whereby the seller transfers the ownership of an object to the buyer and the buyer pays the price for the object.

买卖合同是出卖人转让标的物的所有权于买受人，买受人支付价款的合同。

● **Unless Otherwise**: This expression is more formal than "if not" and "otherwise." 除非

Example 1

Unless otherwise specified in the Contract, the supplied Goods shall be packed by standard protective measures.

除非合同另有规定，（卖方）提供的全部货物，均应按标准的保护措施进行包装。

Example 2

The Contractor shall not subcontract the whole of the Works. Except where otherwise provided by the Contract, the Contractor shall not subcontract any part of the Works without the prior consent of the engineer.

承包人不得将整个工程分包出去。除合同另有规定外无工程师的事先同意，承包人不得将工程的任何部分分包出去。

Example 3

The Contractor shall, unless otherwise provided in the Contract, make his own arrangements for the engagement of all staff and labor, local or other, and for their payment, housing, feeding and transport.

除非合同另有规定，承包人应自行安排从当地或其他地方雇用的所有职员和劳务人员，以及他们的报酬、住宿、膳食和交通。

● **In Accordance with; Under; Pursuant to:** 根据，按照

Example 1

"Permanent Works" means the permanent works to be executed (including Plant) in accordance with the Contract.

"永久工程"是根据合同将实施的永久工程（包括机械设备）。

Example 2

Neither the Consultants nor their Sub-consultants nor the Personnel of either of them shall, either directly or indirectly, engage in such business or professional activities in China as conflict with the activities assigned to them under this Contract.

咨询人、分包咨询人或两类人员，均不能直接或间接地在中国从事与本合同所赋予的活动相冲突的商业或职业活动。

Example 3

"Retention Money" means the aggregate of all monies retained by the Employer

Chapter Nine Translation on Marketing Agreements

pursuant to Sub-Clause 60.2(a).

"保留金"是指业主根据第 60.2（a）款规定留存的所有款项的总额。

● **In Respect of; In Respect Thereof** 涉及，至于，在……方面

Example 1

Prior to making a claim under the performance security, the Employer shall, in every case, notify the Contractor stating the nature of the default in respect of which the claim is to be made.

根据履约保证，提出索赔之前，在任何情况下，业主应通知承包人，针对提出的索赔说明违约的性质。

Example 2

The Employer shall indemnify the Contractor against all claims, proceedings, damages, costs, charges and expenses in respect of the matters (referred to in the exceptions) defined in Sub-Clause 22.2.

业主应保障承包人免除承担属于第 22.2 款规定情况下的所有索赔、诉讼、损害、诉讼费、指控费及其他开支。

Example 3

The Employer shall not be liable to the Contractor for any matter or thing arising out of or in connection with the Contract or execution of the Works, unless the Contractor shall have included a claim in respect thereof in his Final Statement and in the Statement at Completion referred to in Sub-Clause 60.5.

除非承包人在其最终报表中以及在第 60.5 款提及的竣工报表中已经包括索赔事宜，对由合同及工程实施引起的或与之有关的任何问题和事件，雇主不应对承包人负有责任。

● **In the Event that; In the Event of:** 如果，在……情况下

Example 1

In the event that the Contract Price or any other terms of the Contract changes after the issuance of the Letter of Credit (or letter of Guarantee) the Owner shall arrange for such Letter to be amended accordingly as soon as possible after any such change.

如果在信用证（或保函）开出后，合同总价或合同其他条款发生变化，业主应尽快安排对信用证（或保函）进行相应的修改。

Example 2

Either Party hereto may terminate this Agreement in the event of the bankruptcy or insolvency of the other party.

本协议任何一方可以在对方破产或资不抵债的情况下终止本协议。

Sample Translation on a Marketing Agreement

The following is a sample translation of an exclusive distribution agreement:

This Agreement is made and entered into this 15th day of June, 2015, by and between ABC Co., Ltd., a corporation duly organized and existing under the laws of People's Republic of China, with its principal place of business at XXX (hereinafter called seller) and XYZ Co., Ltd., a corporation dully organized and existing under the laws of the United States, with its principal of business at XX (hereinafter called agent), whereby it's mutually agreed as follows:

本协议于 2015 年 6 月 15 日，由 ABC 公司（一家根据中国法律组建并存在的公司，其主营业地在 XXX，以下简称卖方）与 XYZ 公司（一家根据美国法律组建并存在的公司，其主营地在 XX，以下简称代理商）共同签订并一致约定如下：

Article 1 Appointment and Acceptance（委任与接受）

During the effective period of this agreement, seller hereby appoints agent as its exclusive agent to solicit orders for products stipulated in Article 4 from customers in the territory stipulated in Article 3 and agent accepts and assumes such appointment.

在本协议有效期内，卖方指定代理商为本协议第四条项下商品的独家代

Chapter Nine   Translation on Marketing Agreements

理商，在第三条规定的区域内招揽订单。代理商同意并接受上述委任。

Article 2 Agent's Duty（代理商的义务）

Agent shall strictly conform to any and all instructions given by Seller to Agent from time to time and shall not make any representation, warranty, promise, contract, agreement or do any other act binding seller. Seller shall not be held responsible for any acts or failures to act by agent in excess of or contrary to such instructions.

代理商应严格遵守卖方随时给予的任何指令，而且不得代表卖方做出任何担保、承诺以及订立合同、协议或做其他对卖方有约束力的行为。对于代理商违反卖方指令或超出指令范围的一切作为或不作为，卖方不承担任何责任。

Article 3 Territory (代理区域)

The territory covered under this agreement shall be expressly confined to XXX (hereinafter called Territory).

本协议所指的代理区域是：XXX（以下简称区域）。

Article 4 Products (代理商品)

The products covered under this agreement shall be expressly confined to XXX(hereinafter called products).

本协议所指的代理商品是XXX（以下简称商品）。

Article 5 Exclusive Right (排他代理权)

In consideration of the exclusive right herein granted, Seller shall not , directly or indirectly , sell or export products to Territory through other channel than Agent and Agent shall not sell, distribute or promote the sale of any products competitive with or similar to products in Territory and shall not solicit or accept orders for the purpose of selling products outside Territory. Seller shall refer to Agent any

inquiry or order for products Seller may receive from others in Territory during the effective period of this agreement.

基于本协议授予的排他代理权，卖方不得在代理区域内，直接或间接地，通过其他渠道销售、出口代理商品。代理商也不得在代理区域内经销、分销或促销与代理商品类似或有竞争性的商品，也不能招揽或接受以向区域外销售为目的的订单。在本协议有效期内，对来自区域内其他顾客有关代理商品的订单、询价，卖方都应将其转交给代理商。

Article 6 Minimum Transaction (最低交易金额)

In the event that during one year (12months) during the effective period of this Agreement , aggregate payment received by Seller from customers on orders obtained by Agent under this Agreement amounts to less than XXXX, Seller shall have the right to terminated this Agreement by giving thirty(30) day's written notice to Agent.

在本协议有效期内，如果卖方通过代理商每年（12个月）从客户处收到的货款金额低于XXXX，则卖方有权提前30天书面通知代理商解除本协议。

Article 7 Orders (订单)

In soliciting orders, Agent shall adequately advise customers of the general terms and conditions of Seller's sales note or contract note and of any contract being subject to the confirmation of acceptance by Seller. Agent shall immediately dispatch any order received to seller for its acceptance or rejection. The Seller shall have the right to refuse to execute or accept any such orders or any part thereof and the Agent shall not be entitled to any commission in respect of any such rejected order or part thereof refused.

在招揽订单时，代理商应将卖方销售合同的一般交易条件给客户以充分通知，也应告之客户，任何合同的订立都必须经卖方确认。代理商应将收到的订单立即转交卖方，由卖方确定接受与否。卖方有权利拒绝履行或接受代理商转交的订单或订单的一部分，而代理商对于被拒绝的订单或其中一部分，

Chapter Nine Translation on Marketing Agreements

无权要求佣金。

Article 8 Expenses (费用分担)

All expenses and disbursements such as cabling, travelling and other expenses incurred in connection with the sale of products shall be for the account of Agent, unless especially arranged. Further, Agent shall, at his own expenses, maintain office(s), salesman and other sufficient for the performance of the obligation of agent in conformity with any and all instructions given by seller.

除另有约定，所有费用和支出，如电讯费、差旅费以及其他相关销售费用，都应由代理商承担。此外，代理商还应承担维持其办公处所、销售人员以及用于执行卖方有关代理商义务的所有指令而发生的费用。

Article 9 Commission (佣金)

Seller shall pay to Agent commission in XX currency at the rate of XX% of the net invoiced selling price of products on all orders directly obtained by Agent accepted by Seller, such commission shall be payable every six months only after Seller receives the full amount of all payments due to Seller. Payments of such commission shall be made to Agent by way of remittance.

卖方接受代理商直接获得的所有订单后，应按发票净售价XX%，以XX(货币)支付给代理商佣金。佣金在卖方收到全部货款后每六个月以汇款方式支付。

Article 10 Information and Report (商情报告)

Both Seller and Agent shall quarterly and/or on the request of either party furnish information and market report each other to promote the sale of products as much as possible. Agent shall furnish to seller report of inventory, market situation and other commercial activities.

卖方和代理商都应按季度或按对方要求提供信息和市场报告，以尽可能促进商品销售。代理商应向卖方报告商品库存情况、市场状况以及其他商业活动。

Article 11 Sales Promotion（促销）

Agent shall diligently and adequately advertise and promote the sale of products throughout Territory. Seller shall furnish without charge to Agent reasonable quantity of advertising literatures, catalogues, leaflets, folders, and the like as Agent may reasonable require.

在代理区域内，代理商应积极、充分地进行广告宣传以促进商品销售。卖方应向分销商无偿提供一定数量的广告说明书、印刷品、小册子以及代理商合理要求的其他材料。

Article 12 Industrial Property Rights（工业产权）

Agent may use the trade mark of Seller during the effective period of this Agreement only in connection with the sale of products, provided that even after the termination of this Agreement Agent may use the trade market in connection with the sale of products held by it in stock at the time of termination. Agent shall also acknowledge that any and all patterns, trade markets, copyright and other industrial property rights used or embodied in products shall remain to be sole properties of Seller and shall not dispute them in any way. If any infringement being found, Agent shall promptly notify Seller and assist Seller to take steps to protect its right.

在本协议有效期内，代理商可以使用卖方的商标，但仅限于代理商品的销售。本协议终止后，代理商销售库存的代理商品时，仍可使用卖方商标。代理商承认使用于或包含代理商品中的任何专利、商标、版权以及其他工业产权，都属于卖方所有，并不得以任何方式提出异议。一旦发现侵权，代理商应及时通知卖方，并协助卖方采取措施保护卖方的权利。

Article 13 Duration（协议有效期）

This agreement shall enter into force on the signing of both parties. At least three months before the expiration of the agreement, both Seller and Agent shall

Chapter Nine Translation on Marketing Agreements

consult each other for renewal of this Agreement. If the renewal of this Agreement is agreed upon by both parties, this Agreement shall be renewed for another XX year(s)' period under the terms and conditions herein set forth, with amendments if agreed by both parties. Unless this Agreement shall expire on the Xth day of X, XX.

本协议经双方签字生效。在本协议终止前至少3个月，卖方和代理商应共同协商协议的延续。如双方一致同意延续，本协议应在上述各项条款（以及相关修改，若有的话）的基础上，继续有效XX年。否则，本协议将于XX年X月X日终止。

Article 14 Termination (协议的终止)

In case there is any non-performance and/or violation of the terms and conditions under this Agreement by either party during the effective period of this Agreement, the parties hereto shall do their best to settle the matter in question as soon as possible to mutual satisfaction. Unless settlement should be reached within thirty days after notification in writing of the other party, such other party shall have the right to cancel this agreement and the loss and damages sustained thereby shall be indemnified by the party responsible for the non-performance and/or violation. Further in case of bankruptcy or insolvency or liquidation or death and/or reorganization by the third party of the other party, either party has the right to terminate this agreement.

在本协议有效期内，任何一方当事人不履行协议或违反协议条款，双方当事人应力争及时、友好地解决争议以期双方满意。如果在违反方接到书面通知后30日内问题仍无法解决，非违约方有权取消本协议，由此造成的损失和赔偿金概由违约方承担。此外，若协议一方发生破产、清算、死亡和/或被第三方重组，双方均有权终止本协议。

Article 15 Force Majeure (不可抗力)

Either party shall not be responsible for failure or delay to perform all or any part of the obligations under this Agreement, which include: acts of god, government orders or restriction or any other events which could not be predicted at the time of the conclusion of the Agreement and could not be controlled, avoided or overcome by the parties. However, the party affected by the event of force majeure shall inform the other party of its occurrence in writing as soon as possible.

任何一方对因下列原因导致不能或暂时不能履行全部或部分协议义务不负责任。这些原因包括：自然灾害、政府采购或禁令以及其他任何双方在签约时不能预料、无法控制且不能避免和克服的事件。受不可抗力影响的一方应尽快地将发生的情况书面通知对方。

Article 16 Trade Terms and Governing Law（贸易条件与合同准据法）

The trade terms under this agreement shall be governed and interpreted under the provisions of INCOTERMS 2000 and this agreement shall be governed as to all matters including validity, construction, and performance under the laws of People's Republic of China.

本协议的贸易条件适用解释 INCOTERMS 2000。本协议的有效性、缔结及履行受中华人民共和国法律管辖。

Article 17 Arbitration （仲裁）

All disputes arising from the performance of the Agreement should be settled through friendly negotiations. Should no settlement be reached through negotiation, the case shall be submitted for arbitration to the China International Economic and Trade Arbitration Commission (Beijing) and the rules of this commission shall be applied. The award of the arbitration shall be final and binding upon both parties. The arbitration fee shall be borne by the losing party.

对于因履行本协议发生的一切争议，双方应友好协商解决。若无法协商解决，则应提交中国国际经济贸易仲裁委员会（北京分会）根据其仲裁规则进行仲裁。仲裁裁决是最终的，对双方均有约束力。仲裁费用应由败诉方承担。

Chapter Nine   Translation on Marketing Agreements

This agreement shall come into effect immediately after it is signed by both parties in two original copies; each party holds one copy.

本协议由双方代表签字后生效,正本一式两份,双方各执一份。

Chapter Ten

Translation on Breach of Contract Claim

Introduction

The law of contract ("contract law") is an area of civil law (as opposed to criminal law). Contract law is concerned with legal rights and remedies resulting from agreements entered into between individuals or companies.

A contract is therefore basically a promise by one party to another which the law recognizes as enforceable. A breach of contract arises when one party alleges that another party to an agreement has in some way failed to comply with the terms of the agreement. Terms of an agreement may be expressed (i.e., specifically written or stated) or implied. Implied terms are mainly created as a result of established case law or statute. (For example, when a business enters into a contract for the sale of goods, the law of contract implies a term into the contract that the goods will be of *satisfactory quality*.)

The party commencing a breach of contract claim is termed the *Claimant*. The party the claim is brought against is the *Defendant*. A breach of contract claim is commenced by issuing proceedings in court. This is sometimes referred to as "bringing an action."

The usual *remedy* which the court may order for breach of contract is *damages*.

Damages means monetary compensation, usually intended to put the party not at fault in the same position as if the contract had been performed as agreed. (Another remedy the court may grant in certain cases is an injunction.)

A Claim Form

Particulars of Claim

Both of these documents are known as *statements of case*. "Statements of case" is a relatively new legal term for these court documents, which were previously known as "pleadings." You are likely to find that statements of case often contain a certain amount of old-fashioned language. This old-fashioned style of language has traditionally been used when drafting statements of case in order to achieve precision of meaning.

There have been, however, recent reforms encouraging greater use of plain English by lawyers. In particular, a procedural code known as the "Civil Procedure Rules" has introduced some new terminology. We should therefore use plain English whenever possible when drafting statements of case, while still ensuring that the meaning of our drafting is precise and unambiguous.

A range of words in legal English sound rather old-fashioned (such as "ex parte" and "pleading"). Some of these words are still used, having proved through time to be particularly apt and descriptive, thereby having become standard or "stock" phrases. You should, however, always consider carefully whether there is a plain English alternative.

The following table provides some examples. The first column lists words and phrases which have traditionally been used in statements of case over many years. The second column of the table provides a suitable modern English equivalent for the old-style words and phrases in the first column.

Old-Fashioned Language Action	Equivalent Modern Language
action	claim
Anton Piller order	search order
discovery	disclosure
ex parte	without notice (to other parties)
inter-partes hearing	hearing with notice (to other party)
interlocutory hearing	interim (as opposed to final) hearing
interrogatory	request for further information
leave	permission
mandamus order	mandatory order
mareva order (or injunction)	freezing injunction
prohibition order	prohibiting order
request for further and better particulars	request for further information
setting down for trial	listing (scheduling) for tria
specific discovery	specific disclosure
subpoena	witness summons
summons (to commence proceedings)	claim form
summons for directions	case management conference
thereafter/thereinafter	subsequently/then
therein	contained within

The following is a Particulars of Claim.

Chapter Ten   Translation on Breach of Contract Claim

PARTICULARS OF CLAIM PRECEDENT

IN THE HIGH COURT OF JUSTICE

QUEEN'S BENCH DIVISION   CLAIM No. 2007 HC 1829

TRAVELGRAPH LIMITED   [Claimant]

AND

MATRIX PRINTERS LIMITED   [Defendant]

PARTICULARS OF CLAIM

1. The Claimant is and was at all material times a company carrying on business as publishers of maps and tourist guides. The Defendant at all material times carried on business as a manufacturer and seller of printing machines.

2. By a written contract ("the Contract") entered into between the Claimant and the Defendant and signed by both parties on 1 August 2007, the Defendant in the course of its business agreed to manufacture and sell to the Claimant and the Claimant agreed to buy from the Defendant 2 Ultra-Print 123 Series printing machines at a price of £45,000 each.

3. The Contract included an express term that the machines would each be capable of printing at a rate of 100 pages per minute using A4 size paper.

4. The Contract included an implied term that the machines would be of satisfactory quality.

5. Pursuant to the Contract, on 7 August 2007 the Defendant delivered to the Claimant two printing machines ("the delivered machines") which the Claimant installed at its registered office.

6. In breach of the aforesaid express and/or implied term, neither of the delivered machines were capable of printing at a rate exceeding 50 pages per minute.

7. As a result of the matters set out above, the Claimant has suffered loss and damage.

PARTICULARS OF LOSS

Loss of profit

(a) From 7 August 2007 until 8 February 2008:

(i) estimated receipts from warranted output	£200,000
(ii) actual receipts	£100,000
	£100,000

(b) Continuing from 9 February 2008 at the following annual rate:

(i) estimated receipts from warranted output	£400,000
(ii) estimated actual receipts	£200,000
	£200,000

8. Further the Claimant claims interest pursuant to section 35A of the Supreme Court Act 1981 on the amount found to be due to the Claimant at such rate and for such period as the Court thinks fit.

AND the Claimant claims:

(1) Damages

(2) Interest pursuant to section 35A of the Supreme Court Act 1981 to be assessed.

STATEMENT OF TRUTH

The Claimant believes that the facts stated in these Particulars of Claim are true.

Dated this 8th day of February 2008.

Stringwood & Evans, Solicitors, of 18 Bond Street, London.

Solicitors for and on behalf of the Claimant.

Chapter Ten Translation on Breach of Contract Claim

Law Notes

The Particulars of Claim should set out clearly the fundamental details of a breach of contract claim. As illustrated in the example of a Particulars of Claim contained in this chapter, these details should include:

Title of Proceedings

Case Number [provided by the court when the proceedings are issued]

Court [here it is the High Court, Queen's Bench Division]

Full Names of each Party to the Proceedings

Status of each Party [i.e., whether Claimant or Defendant]

The Contract

- Date [1 August 2007]
- Parties [Travelgraph Limited and Matrix Printers Limited]
- Form [i.e., whether written or oral]
- Subject Matter [i.e., what the claim is for]
- Consideration [i.e., a promise to confer a benefit on the other party or to incur a detriment. A contract is usually unenforceable in law unless consideration exists. This is to ensure that all parties to The Contract are providing something in return for what they are receiving. Here, as is commonly the case, there is consideration in the form of the price being paid.]
- Terms of the contract [e.g., price agreed etc. Note that terms of the contract which are specifically material to the claim are set out in paragraphs 3 and 4. Note that it is usual drafting practice to set out express terms before implied terms.]

Breach of the Contract

It is necessary to indicate the term(s) breached, the date(s) and particulars of the breach(es), i.e., what act(s) or omission(s) by the Defendant are being alleged

by the Claimant as having amounted to breach of contract.

Loss and Damage

It is also necessary to particularize the amount and nature of the loss and damage which it is alleged resulted from breach of contract. Even if the court determines that there has been breach of contract, the Claimant also has to establish what is termed causation. Causation is a legal concept whereby only losses caused as a consequence of the breach are recoverable from the Defendant. Such losses are sometimes referred to as having a causal link with the breach.

Remedies

Here the common remedies for breach of contract are indicated, i.e., damages and interest.

Statement of Truth

All statements of case (including claim forms and Particulars of Claim) must contain a statement of truth in wording similar to that indicated here. This will usually be signed by the party whose statement of case it is (i.e., Travelgraph Limited in this case). Note that where the party is a company, the statement of truth would be signed on behalf of the company by a person holding a senior position within the company (such as a director or company secretary) or by the company's lawyer.

Sample Translation on a Chinese Complaint

民事起诉书：

Complaint

原告：

Plaintiff

住所：

Chapter Ten　Translation on Breach of Contract Claim

Domicile

法定代表人：

Legal representative

职务：

Position

被告：

Defendant

住所：

Domicile

法定代表人：

Legal representative

职务：

Position

案由：

Cause of action

买卖合同纠纷：

Sale and purchase contract dispute

请求事项

Claims

1. 判令被告向原告支付已发出货物 [ ] 元人民币的价款以及 [ ] 元人民币的利息，总计 [ ] 元；

2. 判令由被告承担诉讼费用。

1. To order the Defendant to pay to the Plaintiff the due amount of RMB [ ] for the dispatched cargos, plus the interests of RMB [ ] thereon, in the aggregate of RMB [ ].

2. To order the litigation fees to be borne by the Defendant.

事实和理由

Facts and Reasons

被告原系原告在中国 [ ] 地区各种产品的分销商。自 1997 年 9 月至 1998

年10月，原告向其发送了价值总计 [ ] 元人民币的各种产品（见证据一）。

The Defendant was in fact a distributor of the Plaintiff for various products in the territory [ ], China. The Plaintiff had sent products in the aggregate of RMB [ ] to the Defendant from September, 1997 to October, 1998. (see Exhibit I)

上述每笔交易均由被告正式签署和接受（见证据二）。尽管原告多次催讨货款，被告仍未能清偿到期债务。

Each of the transactions mentioned above was duly assigned and accepted by the Defendant (see Exhibit II). Though the Plaintiff has repeatedly demanded the payment, the Defendant fails to liquidate the outstanding debts in due time.

原告认为，因原告与被告之间交易引起的债务应由中国法律管辖。被告在收到上述 [ ] 货物之后拒付约定货款，给原告带来巨大经济损失（见证据三）。因此，根据中国有关法律规定，被告应承担支付违约金的相应民事责任。

It is the Plaintiff's position that any and all indebtedness as a result of the transactions between the Plaintiff and the Defendant shall be under the jurisdiction of China's laws. The Defendant's refusal, after reception of the aforesaid products [ ], to satisfy the agreed amount thereof resulted tremendous economic losses on the part of the Plaintiff (see Exhibit III). Therefore, the Defendant shall, in accordance with relative laws of China, assume corresponding civil liabilities of paying the breach penalty to the Plaintiff.

基于以上原因，根据《中华人民共和国民法通则》第106条和第112条、《中华人民共和国民事诉讼法》第108条及其他适用法律、法规的规定，原告特向贵院提起本案诉讼。

Based on the above-mentioned reason, in accordance with Articles 106 and 112 as set forth in the *PRC General Civil Law*, Article 108 as set forth in the *PRC Civil Procedure Law* and the provisions of other applicable laws and regulations, the Plaintiff hereby files this case with the Court for your adjudication.

此致 [ ] 人民法院

To: [ ] People's Court

原告：[签名或签章]

Chapter Ten　Translation on Breach of Contract Claim

Plaintiff (signature or seal)

委托代理人：

Agent ad litem:

[ ]年[ ]月[ ]

Date：

附：

ATTACHMENTS:

一、原告营业执照副本一份；

1. One copy of the Plaintiff's business license;

二、法定代表人证明原件；

2. One copy of the original Certificate of the legal representative;

三、授权委托书原件；

3. One copy of the original Power of Attorney;

四、证据一：每笔交易发票；

4. Exhibit I: Invoices of each transaction;

五、证据二：每笔交易收据；及

5. Exhibit II: Receipts for each transaction; and

六、证据三：损失清单。

6. Exhibit III: List of loss or losses

Bibliography

1. Akehurst, M. Preparing the authentic English text of the E. E.C. Treaty [A]. In B. A. Wortley (ed.). *An Introduction to the Law of the European Economic Community* [C]. Manchester: Manchester University Press, 1972.
2. Alcaraz, E. & B. Hughes. *Legal Translation Explained* [M]. Shanghai: Shanghai Foreign Language Education Press, 2008.
3. Anderson, B. *Language of the Law* [M]. London: Longman, 1987.
4. Baker, J. *An Introduction to English Legal History (3rd ed.)* [M]. London: Butterworths, 1990.
5. Baker, J. The three languages of the common law [J]. *McGill Law Journal*, 1998, 43: 5.
6. Ballmer, T. & M. Pinkal, *Approaching Vagueness* [M]. Elservier Science Publishers B.V., 1983.
7. Bhatia, V. *Analysing Genre, Language Use in Professional Settings* [M]. London: Longman, 1993.
8. Bhatia, V. Cognitive structuring in legislative provisions [A]. In John Gibbons (ed.). *Language and the* Law [C]. London: Longman Group UK Limited, 1994: 136-155.
9. Black. H. *Black's Law Dictionary* [Z]. St. Paul: West Publishing Company, 1990.
10. Brian, B. *Law, Language, and Legal Determinacy* [M]. Oxford: Oxford University Press, 1996.
11. Bureau of International Information Programs. *Outline of the U.S. Legal*

System [M]. United States Department of State, 2004.

12. Cao, D. *Translating Law* [M]. Shanghai: Shanghai Foreign Language Education Press, 2008.

13. Chen, Ying. "A Project Report on the Translation of Measures of Jiangsu Province on Mediation and Arbitration of Labor and Personnel Disputes" [D]. Nanjing Normal University, 2015.

14. Clanchy, M. *From Memory to Written Record: England 1066–1307* [M]. Oxford: Blackwell, 1993.

15. Dai Weidong & He Zhaoxiong. *A New Concise Course on Linguistics for Students of English* [M]. Shanghai: Shanghai Foreign Language Education Press, 2002.

16. David, R. & J. Brierley, *Major Legal Systems in the World Today* [M]. London: Stevens, 1985.

17. Elizabeth, A. *Oxford Dictionary of Law* [Z]. Oxford: Oxford University Press, 2003.

18. Endicott. T. *Vagueness in Law* [M]. Oxford: Oxford University Press, 2000.

19. Garner. B. *Black's Law Dictionary (9th ed.)* [Z]. St. Paul: West Publishing Co., 2009.

20. Gentzler, E. *Contemporary Transaltion Theory* [M]. Shanghai: Shanghai Foreign Language Education Press, 2004.

21. Gibbons, J. *Forensic Linguistics: An Introduction to Language in the Justice System* [M]. UK: Blackwell Publishing Ltd., 2003.

22. Goodrich, P. *Legal Discourse: Studies in Linguistic, Rhetoric and Legal Analysis* [M]. London: Macmillan,1987.

23. Hart, H. *The Concept of Law* [M]. Oxford: Oxford University Press, 1961.

24. Jackson, B. S. *Semiotics and Legal Theory* [M]. London: Routledge, 1985.

25. Jing, Qinfang. "Cultural Factors and E-C Legal Translation" [D]. Nanjing Normal University, 2011.

26. Joseph, J. E. Indeterminacy, translation and the law [A]. In Marshall Morris (ed.).

Translation and the Law [C]. Amsterdam: John Benjamins, 1995.

27. Joanna Channell, *Vague Language* [M].UK: Oxford University Press, 2000.
28. Kaplan, R. *Cultural Thought Patterns in Intercultural Education* [M]. New York: Lawrence Erlbaum Associates, 2001.
29. Knowles, G. *A Cultural History of the English Language* [M]. Beijing: Peking University Press, 2004.
30. Kramsch, C. *Language and Culture* [M]. Oxford: Oxford University Press, 1998.
31. Kuner, C. The interpretation of multilingual treaties: comparison of texts versus the presumption of similar meaning [J]. *Comparative Law Quarterly*, 1991, 40 (4): 953.
32. Maley, Y. The language of the law [A]. In Jonh Gibbons (ed.). *Language and the Law* [C]. New York: Longman, 1994.
33. Matilla, H. *Comparative Legal Linguistics* [M]. trans. C. Goddard. Aldershot: Ashgate, 2006.
34. McKay, W., Helen E. Charlton. *Legal English—How to Understand and Master the Language of Law* [M]. New York: Pearson Education Limited, 2005.
35. Mellinkoff, D. *The Language of the Law* [M]. Boston and Toronto: Little, Brow and Company, 1990.
36. Mellinkoff, D. *A Dictionary of English Legal Usage* [M]. Beijing: CITIC Publish House,1992.
37. National Adult Literacy Agent. *A Plain English Guide to Legal Terms* [M]. Dublin: National Adult Literacy Agency, 2003.
38. Newmark, P. *Approaches to Translation* [M]. Oxfords and New York: Pergamon, 1981.
39. Nida, E. *Towards a Science of Translating* [M]. Leiden: E. J. Brill, 1964.
40. Nida, E. *Language, Culture, and Translating* [M]. Shanghai: Shanghai Foreign Language Education Press,1993
41. Nida, E. & C. Taber, *The Theory and Practice of Translation* [M]. Leiden: E. J. Brill, 1969.

42. Salmi-Tolone, T. Legal linguistic knowledge and creating and interpreting law in multilingual environment [J]. *Brooklyn Journal of International Law*, 2004, 29(3): 1180-1181.

43. Sarcevic, S. Translation of culture-bound terms in laws [J]. *Multilingua*, 1985, 4(3): 127-133.

44. Sarcevic, S. *New Approach to Legal Translation* [M]. London: Kluwer Law International, 1997.

45. Schroth, P. W. Legal translation [J]. *American Journal of Comparative Law*, 1986, 55-56.

46. Smith, S. A. Culture clash: Anglo-American case law and German civil law in translation [A]. In Marshall Morris (ed.) *Translation and the Law* [C]. Amesterdam: John Benjamins, 1995.

47. Snell-Hornby, M. *Translation Studies, An Integrated Approach* [M]. Amsterdam: Benjamins. 1988.

48. Tabory, M. *Multilingualism in International Law and Institutions* [M]. Alphen aan den Rijin: Sijthoff &Noordoff, 1980.

49. Tallon, D. Le choix des mots au regard des contraintes de traduction[A]. in N. Molfessis (ed.), Les mots de la loi, Paris: Economica 1990.

50. Tetley, W. Mixed jurisdictions: common law vs civil law (codified and uncodified) [J]. *Louisana Law Review,* 2000: 73.

51. Tiersma P. *Legal Language* [M]. Chicago: The University of Chicago Press, 1999.

52. Tiersma, P. The nature of legal language [A]. In John Gibbons & M. Teresa Turell (ed.) *Dimensions of Forensic Linguistics* [C]. Amsterdam/ Philadelphia: John Benjamins Publishing Company, 2008.

53. Toury, G. Translation: a cultural-semiotic perspective [A]. In Tomas A. Sebeok(ed.). *Encyclopaedia Dictionary of Semiotics* [C]. Berlin: Mouton de Gruyter, 1986:1123.

54. Tytler, A. F. *Essay on the Principles of Translation* [M]. Amsterdam: John

Benjamins Publishing Company, 1978.

55. Warrd, Jan de & E. Nida. *From One Language to Another: Functional Equivalence in Bible Translating* [M]. Nashville, Camden and New York: Thomas Nelson Publishers, 1986.

56. Weihofen, H. *Legal Writing Style* [M]. St. Paul : West Publishing Company, 1961.

57. White, J. Law as language: reading law and reading literature [J]. *Texas Law Review*, 1982: 423.

58. Wilss, W. *The Science of Translation: Problems and Methods* [M]. Shanghai: Shanghai Foreign Language Education Press, 2001.

59. Wydick, R.C et al. *California Legal Ethics* [M]. St. Paul: West Publishing Company, 2005.

60. Yu, Yinlei. "Translation of English Legal Texts from the Perspective of Functional Equivalence" [D]. Nanjing Normal University, 2011.

61. Harold J. Berman [伯尔曼].法律与宗教 [M]. 梁治平译, 北京：中国政法大学出版社, 2003.

62. Harold J. Berman [伯尔曼]. 法律与革命——西方法律传统的形成 [M]. 贺卫方, 高鸿钧等译, 北京：法律出版社, 2008.

63. Cao, Zhijian [曹志建]. 功能主义视角下软性法律外宣文本的翻译：问题与对策 [D]. 上海：上海外国语大学, 2012.

64. Chen et al [陈治安等].模糊语言学概论[M]. 重庆: 西南师范大学出版社, 1997.

65. Chen, Hongwei & Li, Yadan [陈宏薇, 李亚丹]. 新编汉英翻译教程[M]. 上海：上海外语教育出版社，2010.

66. Chen, Weizheng & Wu, Shixiong [陈维振, 吴世雄]. 范畴与模糊语义研究[M]. 福州：福建人民出版社, 2002.

67. Chen, Wenling [陈文玲].试论英汉法律术语的不完全对等现象与翻译[J], 山东外语教学, 2004, (04)：100.

68. Chen, Zhongcheng [陈忠诚]. 法窗译话[M]（一版二印）. 北京：中国对外翻译出版公司, 1998a.

69. Chen, Zhongchen[陈忠诚]. 英汉法律用语正误辨析[M]. 北京：法律出版社, 1998b.

70. Chen, Zhongcheng [陈忠诚].法苑译谭[M]. 北京: 中国法制出版社, 2000.

71. Cheng, Sulin [程苏琳].中国对外经贸法律法规中的模糊语英译研究[D]. 桂林：广西师范大学, 2010.

72. Dong, Xiaobo [董晓波]. 略论英语立法语言的模糊与消除[J]. 外语与外语教学, 2004, (2)：60-63.

73. Dong, Xiaobo [董晓波].略论模糊法律语言的语用修辞功能[J].山东商业职业技术学院学报, 2005, (2): 63-65, 85.

74. Dong, Xiaobo [董晓波]. 法律文本翻译[M]. 北京: 对外经济贸易大学出版社, 2011.

75. Dong, Xiaobo [董晓波]. 论英汉法律术语的"对等"翻译[J]. 西安外国语大学学报, 2015, 23,（3）：109.

76. Dong, Xiaobo [董晓波]. 法律翻译为全球治理贡献中国智慧[N]. 中国社会科学报, 2018-06-26.

77. Du, Jinbang [杜金榜]. 从法律语言的模糊性到司法结果的确定性[J]. 现代外语, 2001, (3): 305-310.

78. Du, Jinbang [杜金榜]. 法律语言学[M]. 上海：上海外语教育出版社, 2004.

79. Du, Jinbang [杜金榜]. 法律语言研究新进展[M]. 北京: 对外经济贸易大学出版社, 2010.

80. Du, Jinbang et al. [杜金榜, 张福, 袁亮].中国法律法规英译的问题和解决[J]. 中国翻译, 2004, 25, (3): 72-76

81. Fang, Liufang [方流芳]. 翻译和中文词汇的创新[A]. 法学翻译与中国法的现代化——"美国法律文库暨法学翻译与法律变迁"研讨会纪实[C]. 北京: 中国政法大学出版社, 2005.

82. He et al [何自然等]. 当代语用学[M]. 北京：外语教学与研究出版社, 2004.

83. Hu, Anna [胡安娜]. 文本类型理论与商务文本翻译 [J]. 语文学刊·外语教育教学, 2013, (5):59-61.

84. Hu et al [胡庚申等]．国际商务合同起草与翻译[M]．北京：外文出版社，2002．

85. Jiang, Yue [蒋跃].解构主义的翻译观与语言的模糊性[J].外语教学, 2007, (2): 83-86.

86. Li, Defeng & Hu, Mu [李德凤, 胡牧].法律翻译研究：现状与前瞻[J].中国科技翻译, 2006, (3): 47-51.

87. Li, Fengxia et al. [李凤霞, 张法连, 徐文彬]. 国家战略视域下的法律英语人才培养[J]. 外国语文（双月刊）, 2015, 31, (5): 134-137

88. Li, Jin & Dong, Xiaobo [李晋, 董晓波]. 地方性法规规章翻译规范化和应对措施——基于江苏省法规规章翻译实践的研究[J]. 东南学术, 2015, (5): 225-233.

89. Li, Kexing [李克兴]. 法律英语条件句的写作和翻译[J], 中国翻译, 2008, (4): 71-77.

90. Li, Kexing [李克兴]. 论法律文本的静态对等翻译 [J]. 外语教学与研究, 2010, (1): 59-65.

91. Li, Kexing & Zhang, Xinhong [李克兴、张新红].法律文本与法律翻译[M]. 北京: 中国对外翻译出版公司, 2006.

92. Li, Wenge & Wu, Baizhen [李文戈, 武柏珍]. 翻译视野中的语言模糊性[J]. 外语学刊, 2004, (3): 84-87.

93. Li, Yunxing [李运兴]. 语际翻译中的文化因素[A]. 载郭建中（编）文化与翻译[C]. 北京: 中国对外翻译出版公司, 2000.

94. Li, Ziheng [李自恒]. A Dual Equivalence Translation Model for Legal Texts Based on Nida's Functional Equivalence Theory [D]. 四川：电子科技大学, 2009.

95. Liang, Lihong [梁丽红]. 英语法律文书的词汇句式特点及翻译策略[J]. 湖北函授大学学报, 2012, (7): 138-139.

96. Liang, Zhiping [梁治平]. 法律的文化解释（增订本）[M]. 北京：生活·读书·新知三联书店, 1994.

97. Lin, Kenan & Ji, Minhwen [林克难、籍明文]. 法律文书中"的"字结构翻译

探讨[J]. 上海科技翻译, 2002, (3): 20-22.

98. Liu, Liai [刘利艾]. 英语法律文本的语言特点与翻译[D]. 上海: 上海师范大学, 2009.

99. Liu, Miqing [刘宓庆]. 文体与翻译(第二版) [M]. 北京: 中国对外翻译出版公司, 2012.

100. Lu, Min [卢敏]. 英语法律文本的语言特点与翻译 [M]. 上海：上海交通大学出版社, 2008.

101. Lv, Zixian [吕自先]. 文本类型、功能理论视角下的商务文本翻译策略 [J]. 商务必读, 2014, (1): 166-167.

102. Ma, Hongjun [马红军]. 翻译补偿手段的分类与应用——兼评Hawkes《红楼梦》英译本的补偿策略[J]. 外语与外语教学, 2003, (10): 37-39.

103. Ma, Huijuan [马会娟]. 奈达翻译理论研究[M]. 北京: 外语教学与研究出版社, 2003.

104. Ma, Li [马莉]. 法律语言翻译的文化制约[M]. 北京: 法律出版社, 2009.

105. Qiu, Guixi [邱贵溪]. 论法律文件翻译的若干原则[J]. 中国科技翻译, 2000, (2): 14-17.

106. Qu, Wensheng [屈文生]. 中国法律术语对外翻译面临的问题与成因反思——兼谈近年来我国法律术语译名规范化问题[J]. 中国翻译, 2012, (6): 68-75.

107. Shi, Bingyun [施冰芸]. 全译视域下的商务翻译补偿 [J]. 广西青年干部学院学报, 2015, (2): 77-80.

108. Shi, Dingxu [石定栩]. "的"和"的"字结构[J]. 当代语言学, 2008, (4): 298-307.

109. Song, Lei [宋雷]. 法律词语空缺及翻译对策[J]. 西南民族大学学报, 2006, (01): 233-237.

110. Summers, D. [萨默斯]. 朗文当代英语大辞典（英英.英汉双解）[Z]. 朱原等译. 北京：商务印书馆, 2004.

111. Sun, Wanbiao [孙万彪]. 英汉法律翻译教程[M]. 上海: 上海外语教育出版社, 2003.

112. Tang, Hongbo [汤洪波]. 法律英语的模糊性及其翻译策略[J]. 科技信息, 2011, (36): 532-533.

113. Wang, Fengxin [王逢鑫]. 英语模糊语法[M]. 北京: 外文出版社, 2001.

114. Wang, Ning [王宁]. 翻译研究的文化转向[M]. 北京: 清华大学出版社, 2009.

115. Wang, Zuoliang & Ding, Wangdao [王佐良, 丁往道]. 英语文体学引论[M]. 北京: 外语教学与研究出版社, 1987.

116. Wei, Jin [魏瑾]. 文化介入与翻译的文本行为研究[M]. 上海: 上海交通大学出版社, 2009.

117. Wu, Qiaofang [伍巧芳]. 法律语言模糊性的法理分析[J]. 江西社会科学, 2009, (6): 244-248.

118. Xiao, Yunshu [肖云枢]. 英语语法特点初探 [J]. 外语教学, 2000, 21(4)：48-55.

119. Xiao, Yunshu [肖云枢]. 英汉法律术语的特点、词源及翻译[J]. 中国翻译, 2001, (3) : 44-47.

120. Xie, Yanhong [谢燕鸿]. 法律英语翻译的准确性与模糊性 [J]. 双语学习·翻译交流, 2007, (9): 159-161.

121. Xiong, Demi [熊德米]. 模糊性法律语言翻译的特殊要求[J]. 外语学刊, 2008, (6): 113-116.

122. Xiong, Demi & Xiong, Shudan [熊德米, 熊姝丹]. 法律翻译的特殊原则[J]. 西南政法大学学报, 2011, (4):128-135.

123. Xu, Duo [许多]. 论翻译硕士法律翻译人才培养的困境与对策[J]. 中国外语, 2017, 14(2): 14-20.

124. Xu, Peng [许鹏]. 国际科技合作英文协议的句法特点及翻译[J]. 中国科技翻译, 2014, (4): 14-17, 23.

125. Xu, Xingyan [徐行言]. 中西文化比较[M]. 北京: 北京大学出版社, 2004.

126. Yang, Xianyu [杨贤玉].英汉文化差异与翻译[J]. 西安外国语学院学报, 2001, (4): 70-72.

127. Zhang, Falian [张法连]. 法律英语翻译[M]. 济南: 山东大学出版社, 2009.

128. Zhang, Falian [张法连]. 英美法律术语汉译策略探究[J]. 中国翻译, 2016,

(2):100-104.

129. Zhang, Falian [张法连]. "一带一路"背景下法律翻译教学与人才培养问题探究[J]. 翻译教学, 2018, (2): 31-35.

130. Zhang, Mingjie [张明杰]. 论法律术语翻译的规范化[J]. 贵州大学学报（社会科学版）, 2015, (1): 165-168.

131. Zhang, Wenxian [张文显]. 主持人开场白[A]. 法学翻译与中国法的现代化——"美国法律文库暨法学翻译与法律变迁"研讨会纪实[C]. 北京：中国政法大学出版社, 2005.

132. Zhang, Xinhong [张新红]. 汉语立法语篇的言语行为分析[J]. 现代外语, 2000, (3): 283-295.

133. Zhang, Xinhong [张新红]. 文本类型与法律文本[J]. 现代外语, 2001, (2): 192-200.

134. Zhang, Zhongqiu [张中秋]. 中西法律文化比较研究[M]. 南京: 南京大学出版社, 1999.

135. Zhao, Junfeng & Luo, Wenqi [赵军峰, 罗雯琪]. 国内法律翻译教材现状分析(1992-2012) [J]. 中国翻译, 2012, (5): 48-52.

136. Zhao, Zhenjiang & Fu, Zitang [赵震江, 付子堂]. 现代法理学[M]. 北京: 北京大学出版社, 1999.

137. Zhu, Dexi [朱德熙]. 自指和转指——汉语名词化标记"的、者、所、之"的语法功能和语义功能[J]. 方言, 1983, (1): 16-31.

138. Zhu, Dingchu [朱定初]. 美国法律新词试译[J]. 中国翻译, 2000, (4): 47.

139. Zhu, Dingchu [朱定初]. 评复旦大学《法律英语》中的译注——兼谈法律专门术语翻译的基本原则[J].中国翻译, 2002, (3): 65-70.

140. Zou, Yuhua [邹玉华]. 论立法文本中"有下列情形（行为）之一的"句式的规范[J]. 语言文字应用, 2008, (4): 100-107.

141. http://www.diffen.com/difference/Civil_Law_vs_Common_Law, 2019-03-24.